Being a Writer™

Funding for Developmental Studies Center has been generously provided by:

The Annenberg Foundation, Inc.

The Atlantic Philanthropies (USA) Inc.

Booth Ferris Foundation

The Robert Bowne Foundation, Inc.

The Annie E. Casey Foundation

Center for Substance Abuse Prevention
　U.S. Department of Health and Human Services

The Danforth Foundation

The DuBarry Foundation

The Ford Foundation

Google Inc.

William T. Grant Foundation

Evelyn and Walter Haas, Jr. Fund

Walter and Elise Haas Fund

The Horace Hagedorn Foundation

J. David and Pamela Hakman Family Foundation

Hasbro Children's Foundation

Charles Hayden Foundation

The William Randolph Hearst Foundations

Clarence E. Heller Charitable Foundation

The William and Flora Hewlett Foundation

The James Irvine Foundation

The Robert Wood Johnson Foundation

Walter S. Johnson Foundation

Ewing Marion Kauffman Foundation

W.K. Kellogg Foundation

John S. and James L. Knight Foundation

Lilly Endowment, Inc.

Longview Foundation

Louis R. Lurie Foundation

The John D. and Catherine T. MacArthur Foundation

A.L. Mailman Family Foundation, Inc.

The MBK Foundation

Mr. and Mrs. Sanford N. McDonnell

Mendelson Family Fund

Charles Stewart Mott Foundation

National Institute on Drug Abuse,
　National Institutes of Health

National Science Foundation

New York Life Foundation

Nippon Life Insurance Foundation

Karen and Christopher Payne Foundation

The Pew Charitable Trusts

The Pinkerton Foundation

The Rockefeller Foundation

Louise and Claude Rosenberg Jr. Family Foundation

The San Francisco Foundation

Shinnyo-en Foundation

Silver Giving Foundation

The Spencer Foundation

Spunk Fund, Inc.

W. Clement & Jessie V. Stone Foundation

Stuart Foundation

The Stupski Family Foundation

The Sulzberger Foundation, Inc.

Surdna Foundation, Inc.

John Templeton Foundation

U.S. Department of Education

The Wallace Foundation

Wells Fargo Bank

VOLUME **2**
TEACHER'S MANUAL

Grade 2

Being a Writer™

I love my hair. I can put in anyanway a want.

DEVELOPMENTAL
STUDIES CENTER™

First edition published 2007.

Being a Writer is a trademark of Developmental Studies Center.

Developmental Studies Center wishes to thank the following authors, agents, and publishers for their permission to reprint materials included in this program. Many people went out of their way to help us secure these rights and we are very grateful for their support. Every effort has been made to trace the ownership of copyrighted material and to make full acknowledgment of its use. If errors or omissions have occurred, they will be corrected in subsequent editions, provided that notification is submitted in writing to the publisher.

Excerpts from "Answers to Kids' Frequently Asked Questions" from www.koko.com. Reprinted by permission of The Gorilla Foundation. All rights reserved. Excerpt from *First Year Letters*, text copyright © 2003 by Julie Danneberg. Illustrations copyright © 2003 by Judy Love. Used with permission by Charlesbridge Publishing, Inc. All rights reserved. "Tree House" from *Where the Sidewalk Ends* copyright © 2004 by Evil Eye Music, Inc. Reprinted with permission from the estate of Shel Silverstein and HarperCollins Children's Books. Used by permission of HarperCollins Publishers. "Boa Constrictor" from *Where the Sidewalk Ends* copyright © 2004 by Evil Eye Music, Inc. Reprinted with permission from the estate of Shel Silverstein and HarperCollins Children's Books. Used by permission of HarperCollins Publishers. "The Coyote" from *mammalabilia*, text copyright © 2000 by Douglas Florian, reprinted by permission of Harcourt, Inc. This material may not be reproduced in any form or by any means without the prior written permission of the publisher. "The Tiger" from *mammalabilia*, text copyright © 2000 by Douglas Florian, reprinted by permission of Harcourt, Inc. This material may not be reproduced in any form or by any means without the prior written permission of the publisher. "Knoxville, Tennessee" from *Black Feeling, Black Talk, Black Judgment* by Nikki Giovanni, copyright © 1968, 1970 by Nikki Giovanni. Reprinted by permission of HarperCollins Publishers. "Lettuce"/"Lechuga" text copyright © 1997 by Alma Flor Ada, English translation copyright © 1997 by Rosa Zubizarreta, from *Gathering the Sun: An Alphabet in Spanish and English*. Used by permission of HarperCollins Publishers. "Peaches"/"Duraznos" text copyright © 1997 by Alma Flor Ada, English translation copyright © 1997 by Rosa Zubizarreta, from *Gathering the Sun: An Alphabet in Spanish and English*. Used by permission of HarperCollins Publishers. "My Baby Brother" from *Fathers, Mothers, Sisters, Brothers* by Mary Ann Hoberman. Text copyright © 1991 by Mary Ann Hoberman; illustrations copyright © 1991 by Marilyn Hafner. Used by permission of Little, Brown and Co. "Wind Song" from *I Feel the Same Way* by Lilian Moore. Copyright © 1966, 1967 Lilian Moore. Used by permission of Marian Reiner. "Weather" by Aileen Fisher from *Always Wondering* by Aileen Fisher. Copyright © 1991 by Aileen Fisher. Used by permission of Marian Reiner. "Fish" by Mary Ann Hoberman from *Read-Aloud Rhymes for the Very Young*. Copyright © 1986 by Mary Ann Hoberman. Reprinted by permission of Gina Maccoby Literary Agency. "Clouds" by Christina G. Rossetti appears in *Sing a Song of Popcorn* copyright © 1988, selected by Beatrice Schenk de Regniers, Eva Moore, Mary Michaels White, and Jan Carr, and published by Scholastic, Inc. "Rain Poem" by Elizabeth Coatsworth, used by permission of Paterson Marsh Ltd on behalf of the estate of Elizabeth Coatsworth. "The Steam Shovel" by Rowena Bennett, copyright © Rowena Bennett. Reproduced by permission of the author.

A special thanks to Donald Murray (who passed away December 30, 2006) for the wonderful assortment of author quotations that he gathered in his book *shoptalk: learning to write with writers* published by Boynton/Cook Publishers in 1990.

Developmental Studies Center
2000 Embarcadero, Suite 305
Oakland, CA 94606-5300
(800) 666-7270, fax: (510) 464-3670
www.devstu.org

ISBN-13: 978-1-59892-304-9
ISBN-10: 1-59892-304-8

Printed in the United States of America

3 4 5 6 7 8 9 10 MLY 16 15 14 13 12 11 10

TABLE OF CONTENTS

Nonfiction

Unit 4 Nonfiction

During this five-week unit, the students explore and write nonfiction. They learn that nonfiction authors write about subjects that interest them, and that they ask and answer questions and make careful observations. The students write questions, facts, functional nonfiction, and expository nonfiction. They each select a piece of writing and take it through the writing process. Socially, the students learn discussion prompts to help them build on one another's thinking. They ask for and give help and feedback respectfully.

Development Across the Grades

Grade	Nonfiction Topics and Genre	Research	Skills and Conventions
2	• Writing questions, observations, notes, facts, and other true information • Exploring text features (e.g., preface, table of contents, glossary)	• Listening to short passages of text and saying what was learned • Guided writing of brief notes about what was learned	• Capitalizing the beginnings of sentences and using periods at the ends • Using question marks • Listening for periods
3	• Selecting an **animal** to research and write about • Q&A, ABC, and other formats for nonfiction • Tables of contents • Illustrations and captions	• Preresearch writing • Generating questions • Taking notes • Organizing information by subtopic (e.g., habitat, physical characteristics, food)	• Commas in a series • Apostrophes to show possession • Listening for periods
4	• Selecting a **country** to research and write about • Q&A, pattern, and other formats for nonfiction • Tables of contents • Maps and diagrams	• Preresearch writing • Narrowing research focus • Taking notes • Organizing information by subtopic (e.g., geography, climate, clothing, food)	• Various uses of commas • Apostrophes to show possession • Capitalizing languages, religions, holidays • Listening for periods
5	• Selecting **any nonfiction topic** to research and write about • Exploring different ways to communicate information • Sidebars, glossaries, and other text features	• Preresearch writing • Narrowing research focus • Taking notes • Organizing information by subtopics that are appropriate to the topic	• Transition words (conjunctions) • Citing resources in a bibliography • Listening for periods

UNIT OVERVIEW

WEEK	DAY 1	DAY 2	DAY 3	DAY 4
1	**Exploring Nonfiction:** *Koko's Kitten* **Focus:** • Introducing nonfiction • Writing questions	**Exploring Nonfiction:** *Koko's Kitten* **Focus:** • Writing about Koko • Writing freely	**Exploring Nonfiction:** "Answers to Kids' Frequently Asked Questions About Koko" **Focus:** • Writing about a partner	**Exploring Nonfiction:** *How to Be a Friend* **Focus:** • Writing about how to be a friend • Drawing illustrations to add to text
2	**Exploring Nonfiction** **Focus:** • Writing observations about paper • Using written observations to play a game	**Exploring Nonfiction:** *Paper* **Focus:** • Writing facts and questions about paper • Writing about paper used in the classroom	**Exploring Nonfiction:** *Paper* **Focus:** • Learning discussion prompts • Writing about an experiment and paper use	**Exploring Nonfiction:** *Paper* **Focus:** • Writing about an experiment • Sharing writing in groups of four
3	**Exploring Nonfiction:** *Polar Lands* **Focus:** • Writing information and questions about the polar lands	**Exploring Nonfiction:** *Polar Lands* **Focus:** • Writing about sea animals in the polar lands	**Exploring Nonfiction:** *Polar Lands* **Focus:** • Writing facts about the people of the polar lands • Listing topics	**Exploring Nonfiction** **Focus:** • Choosing topics and writing about the polar lands
4	**Exploring Nonfiction:** *How Do You Know It's Winter?* **Focus:** • Writing about winter	**Exploring Nonfiction:** *Recess at 20 Below* **Focus:** • Writing about spring, summer, or fall	**Exploring Nonfiction and Conferring in Pairs** **Focus:** • Adding descriptions • Giving feedback about what more they want to know	**Selecting Drafts and Conferring in Pairs** **Focus:** • Selecting drafts • Giving feedback • Adding to drafts
5	**Informal Proofreading and Conferring in Pairs** **Focus:** • Proofreading for spelling, punctuation, and capitalization • Giving feedback	**Writing Final Versions** **Focus:** • Exploring illustrations and diagrams • Writing and illustrating final versions	**Publishing** **Focus:** • Completing final versions • Making books	**Publishing** **Focus:** • Sharing from the Author's Chair • Writing freely

UNIT 4: NONFICTION

Koko's Kitten
by Dr. Francine Patterson, photographs by Ronald H. Cohn
(Scholastic Inc., 1985)

Koko, a gorilla that uses sign language to communicate, asks for a kitten for her birthday.

Excerpt

"Answers to Kids' Frequently Asked Questions About Koko"
(see page 324)

Learn interesting facts about Koko through answers written in response to children's questions.

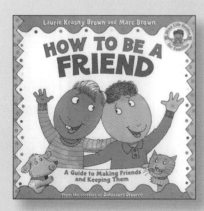

How to Be a Friend: A Guide to Making Friends and Keeping Them
by Laurie Krasny Brown and Marc Brown
(Little, Brown and Company, 1998)

This guide helps children learn ways to be a friend.

Writing Focus

- Students hear and discuss nonfiction.

- Students explore features of nonfiction books.

- Students write questions, facts, expository nonfiction, and functional nonfiction.

- Students draw illustrations that correspond or add to their writing.

Social Focus

- Students act in fair and caring ways.

- Students build the writing community.

- Students express interest in and appreciation for one another's writing.

DO AHEAD

- Prior to Day 1, decide how you will randomly assign partners to work together during this unit. See the front matter in volume 1 for suggestions about assigning partners randomly (page xiii) and for considerations for pairing English Language Learners (page xxvii).

- Prior to Day 1, consider previewing *Koko's Kitten* with your English Language Learners. Read it aloud and show and discuss the photographs, or have the students flip through it on their own. (See pages 307, 308, and 312 for suggested ELL vocabulary.)

TEACHER AS WRITER

"I like to come away from reading a book with the feeling that I've learned something. That's why I like nonfiction."
— *Gail Gibbons*

In your notebook, jot a list of facts about yourself—facts that best define who you are and what interests you—or about any topic you know something about. Then use the facts to write an autobiographical sketch or to tell about the subject you've chosen.

Day 1

Materials

- *Koko's Kitten*
- Chart paper and a marker

Exploring Nonfiction

In this lesson, the students:

- Work with a new partner
- Hear and discuss nonfiction
- Discuss a preface
- Write questions about Koko
- Ask for and give help respectfully

About Nonfiction Writing at Grade 2

The first four weeks of this unit immerse the students in the nonfiction genre. They hear, read, and discuss nonfiction about diverse topics including a gorilla named Koko, paper, and the seasons of the year. They ask and write questions, and they take notes about things they observe closely. They are introduced to research skills as they hear or read short passages of text and are guided in taking notes about what they have learned. This very informal introduction to research and taking notes lays the foundation for more formal instruction in these skills in later grades.

At the end of Week 4, the students review the various pieces of nonfiction they wrote during the unit and pick one piece to complete and publish. In Week 5, they informally revise, proofread, and publish their pieces.

GETTING READY TO WRITE

▶ 1 Pair Students and Introduce Nonfiction

Teacher Note ▶

The partners you assign today will stay together for the unit.

Making Meaning® Teacher

You can either have the students work with their current *Making Meaning* partner or assign them a different partner for the writing lessons.

Randomly assign partners (see "Do Ahead" on page 305). Gather the class with partners sitting together, facing you. Have them bring their notebooks with them.

Explain that during the past few weeks the students heard and wrote fiction stories, stories that are made up using the imagination. Explain that in the coming weeks, partners will work together to explore a different kind of writing, called *nonfiction*. Explain that nonfiction is not made-up or imaginary, but gives true information about something.

2 ▶ Read Part of *Koko's Kitten* Aloud

Show the cover of *Koko's Kitten* and read the title and the names of the author and photographer aloud. Explain that you will read this piece of nonfiction aloud, and invite the students to think as they listen about what makes this a nonfiction book.

Show the preface on pages 4–5, and explain that sometimes authors write a preface at the beginning of a book to give the reader some information and introduce the book. Read the preface aloud, clarifying vocabulary as you read.

Suggested Vocabulary

capable of telling: able to tell (p. 4)

graduate-school project: project done in a school for adults (p. 4)

gibbons: types of apes (p. 4)

lecture: talk by an expert (p. 4)

represent: stand for (p. 5)

documented: written about (p. 5)

enlightened, and inspired me: gave me knowledge, and made me feel excited (p. 5)

ELL Vocabulary

English Language Learners may benefit from discussing additional vocabulary, including:

was very impressed: thought it was great (p. 5)

gave his consent: said yes (p. 5)

Ask and briefly discuss:

Q *What did you learn about Koko from this preface?*

Students might say:

"Koko is a real gorilla."

"The author really works with Koko."

"This story really happened. It isn't made-up."

Q *Now that you've heard the preface, what are you are wondering about? Turn to your partner.*

Signal for the students' attention and explain that you will read part of *Koko's Kitten*. Invite them to listen for information about their questions. Read pages 7–17 aloud, showing the photographs and clarifying vocabulary as you read.

Suggested Vocabulary

durable: able to last for a long time (p. 9)

vinyl: material similar to plastic (p. 9)

tabby: cat that has stripes or other patterns in its coat (p. 12)

ELL Vocabulary

English Language Learners may benefit from discussing additional vocabulary, including:

assortment: collection (p. 9)

abandoned: left alone (p. 12)

cradled: held closely (p. 14)

permanent: lasting or regular (p. 14)

accustomed to: used to (p. 17)

unsupervised: with no person there (p. 17)

▶ 3 Discuss the Reading and List Questions

Ask and briefly discuss:

Q *What have you learned about Koko so far?*

 **Q** *What new questions do you have about Koko? Turn to your partner.*

Call on two or three volunteers to share their questions, and record them on a sheet of chart paper entitled "Questions About Koko." Point out that you are using a question mark to punctuate the end of each question.

Teacher Note ▶

If students have difficulty generating questions, stimulate their thinking by asking and listing questions like those in the diagram on the next page; then ask, "What other questions do you have?"

> ## Questions About Koko
>
> Are Koko and All Ball still friends?
>
> Does Koko have any gorilla friends?
>
> How did Koko learn sign language?

After recording two or three questions on the chart, explain that during writing time partners will continue to talk about their questions and write a list of questions in their own writing notebooks. Encourage the students to help each other write.

WRITING TIME

4▶ Write Questions

Explain that partners will talk softly to each other during writing time today. Have partners move to sit together at desks. Have them discuss and write questions for 10–15 minutes. Join the students in writing for a few minutes; then walk around and observe.

Signal to let the students know when writing time is over. Have the students review the questions they wrote and check to see that they used a question mark at the end of each sentence.

SHARING AND REFLECTING

5▶ Reflect on Helping Each Other

Ask and briefly discuss:

Q *What is one way your partner helped you today?*

◀ **Teacher Note**

If you notice that a number of pairs are struggling to write questions, call for the students' attention and have a few volunteers share the questions they have written. You might also ask questions to stimulate the students' thinking, such as:

Q *What would you like to know about how Koko lives?*

Q *What would you like to know about Koko's favorite things?*

Add the students' questions to the "Questions About Koko" chart; then have pairs resume their work together for a few more minutes.

Share Questions

Ask:

Q *What is something you wonder about Koko?*

Have several volunteers share their questions, and list them on the "Questions About Koko" chart. Explain that the class will hear more about Koko over the next few days.

Teacher Note

Save the "Questions About Koko" chart to use on Days 2 and 3.

Day 2

Exploring Nonfiction

In this lesson, the students:

- Hear and discuss nonfiction
- Write about Koko as a class
- Generate more questions about Koko
- Write freely

GETTING READY TO WRITE

1 ▶ Review *Koko's Kitten*

Gather the class with partners sitting together, facing you. Have them bring their writing notebooks with them.

Review that yesterday the students heard part of *Koko's Kitten*, a nonfiction book. Ask and briefly discuss:

Q *What do you remember about the first part of* Koko's Kitten?

Q *What makes* Koko's Kitten *a nonfiction book?*

Remind the students that they wrote questions about Koko. Briefly review the "Questions About Koko" chart, and then have them quietly review the questions they wrote in their notebooks.

2 ▶ Read the Rest of *Koko's Kitten* Aloud

Explain that today you will read the rest of *Koko's Kitten* aloud. Invite the students to listen for information about their questions as you read. Read pages 18–32 aloud, clarifying vocabulary as you read.

Materials

- *Koko's Kitten*
- "Questions About Koko" chart from Day 1
- Lined chart paper and a marker

FACILITATION TIP

During this unit, practice **asking facilitative questions** during class discussions to help the students build on one another's thinking and respond directly to one another, not just to you. After a student comments, ask the class questions such as:

Q *Do you agree or disagree with [Deborah]? Why?*

Q *What questions can we ask [Deborah] about what she said?*

Q *What can you add to what [Deborah] said?*

Suggested Vocabulary

aggressive: eager to start a fight (p. 18)

obnoxious: very rude and unpleasant (p. 18)

ear mites: tiny bugs that live in the ear (p. 21)

perceptions: things she understands (p. 22)

epilogue: section of a book that tells what happens after the story (p. 32)

ELL Vocabulary

English Language Learners may benefit from discussing additional vocabulary, including:

separated: taken away (p. 18)

affection: love (p. 24)

sympathy: sadness and support (p. 28)

breeder: person who raises animals (p. 30)

Ask and briefly discuss:

Q *What did you learn about Koko from today's reading?*

Q *What feelings did you have as you listened?*

Q (Point to the "Questions About Koko" chart.) *What questions on our list did we learn something about?*

WRITING TIME

 Write a Shared Nonfiction Piece About Koko

Explain that you will lead the class in writing a short nonfiction piece about what they have learned about Koko. Title a sheet of lined chart paper "Koko: A Special Gorilla." Use "Think, Pair, Share" to have partners first think about and then discuss:

 Q *What are some things we have learned about Koko that we can include in our nonfiction piece?* [pause] *Turn to your partner.*

Signal for the students' attention and have a few volunteers share their thinking with the class. Ask the students to watch as you write the first one or two sentences of the piece (see the diagram for ideas). Write the sentences and then use the students' suggestions to continue to add a few more sentences. Be ready to restate the students' ideas as complete sentences, if necessary. Prompt the students with questions such as:

Q *What sentence shall I write next?*

Q *What else can we write about [Koko's friendship with All Ball]?*

Q *What sentence might make sense after this one?*

As you write, model using the word wall, approximating spelling, and using appropriate punctuation. When you finish writing, reread the piece together as a class.

Teacher Note

You may need to remind the students that they are writing nonfiction—true information they have learned about Koko, rather than things they imagine about Koko.

> ### Koko: A Special Gorilla
>
> Koko is a special gorilla. She can talk using sign language. Dr. Francine Patterson takes care of her and shows her the signs.
>
> Koko loves cats and asked for one as a present. She met three kittens. Koko picked a cat without a tail and named him "All Ball."
>
> Koko was very gentle with All Ball. One day he was hit by a car and died. Koko was very sad. Then, Koko got a new kitten. She named him "Lipstick."

SHARING AND REFLECTING

4▶ Reflect on Questioning as Part of Writing Nonfiction

Review that the students have asked questions and learned about Koko, and they have written about Koko as a class. Ask:

Q *Now that you have begun to learn and write about Koko, what other questions do you have about her?*

Add any new questions to the "Questions About Koko" chart. Point out that nonfiction authors often end up having many more questions about their topic after they start writing than they did when they began, and that this is a natural part of the nonfiction writing process.

Explain that the students will find out more about Koko and continue to explore nonfiction tomorrow.

FREE WRITING TIME

5▶ Write Freely

Explain that the students will have some time now to write freely about anything they choose. They may continue to write more questions about Koko, write a list of nonfiction topics they are interested in, or write about anything else they choose. Ask:

 Q *What might you write about today? Turn to your partner.*

Have a few volunteers share their ideas, and then have the students write freely for 10–15 minutes.

Day 3

Exploring Nonfiction

In this lesson, the students:

* Hear, read, and discuss nonfiction
* Write interview questions
* Interview and write about their partner
* Get to know each other
* Ask for and give help respectfully

GETTING READY TO WRITE

1 Read "Answers to Kids' Frequently Asked Questions About Koko"

Gather the class with partners sitting together, facing you. Have them bring their notebooks and *Student Writing Handbooks* with them. Remind them that this week they heard *Koko's Kitten*, a true story about a gorilla named Koko. Direct their attention to the "Questions About Koko" chart and review their questions. Ask and briefly discuss:

Q *Which questions were answered in* Koko's Kitten? *Which questions do we still need answers for?*

Explain that the students will read some questions and answers about Koko from her website to see if any more of their questions are answered. Have them turn to "Answers to Kids' Frequently Asked Questions About Koko" on *Student Writing Handbook* page 6, and invite them to follow along as you read it aloud.

Read the questions and answers aloud, clarifying vocabulary as you read. Explain that "Penny" is Dr. Patterson's nickname. You might also stop to figure out Koko's age from her birth date (July 4, 1971).

Materials

* "Answers to Kids' Frequently Asked Questions About Koko" (see page 324)
* "Questions About Koko" chart
* *Student Writing Handbook* page 6
* Chart paper and a marker
* *Assessment Resource Book*

◀ **Teacher Note**

"Answers to Kids' Frequently Asked Questions About Koko" comes from the website www. koko.org. You might want to check the website to see if there are any new questions or if any of the answers have changed over time.

Suggested Vocabulary

nettles: plants with sharp leaves and stinging spines (p. 324)

insect larvae: baby insects that look like worms (p. 324)

organic: grown without chemicals (p. 324)

gourmet tofu dishes: special foods made with tofu, a soft, cheeselike food made from soybeans (p. 324)

ELL Vocabulary

English Language Learners may benefit from discussing additional vocabulary, including:

Humane Society: organization that takes care of stray animals (p. 325)

molding: making or forming (p. 325)

In pairs and as a class, briefly discuss:

 Q *What is something you learned about Koko? Turn to your partner.*

Q (Point to the "Questions About Koko" chart.) *What questions did this writing help us answer?*

 Model Writing Questions and Interviewing a Partner

Point out that the students have learned many facts about Koko by asking questions and reading for answers. Explain that today they will ask questions to learn facts about another interesting subject, their partner. Afterward, they will share something they learned about their partner with the class.

Ask the students to watch as you model what they will do. On a sheet of chart paper entitled "Questions About My Partner," write three questions to ask a partner, leaving space beneath each question to write an answer.

Questions About My Partner

Where were you born?

How many brothers and sisters do you have?

What do you like to do on weekends?

Select a volunteer as your partner. Model asking the first question. After listening to your partner's answer, explain that an answer to a question often leads to more questions. Model asking one or two follow-up questions to get more information.

Ask and briefly discuss as a class:

Q *What other follow-up questions could I ask my partner about [where she was born]?*

With your partner's help, write an answer for the first question on the chart, including information gleaned from the follow-up questions.

Repeat this process with the two remaining questions.

◀ **Teacher Note**

For example, the first question you ask your partner might be "Where were you born?" You might follow up with questions such as "When did you move here?" and "What do you remember about [China]?"

▶3 **Think Before Writing**

Explain that today the students will write at least three questions to ask their partner, and then they will interview their partner and write answers to their questions. At the end of writing time, they will share something interesting they wrote about their partner with the class. Ask:

Q *What is one question you could ask your partner to learn an interesting fact about him or her?*

Have a few volunteers suggest questions. Remind the students that after each question they write, they need to leave enough space to write the information they learn from the question.

WRITING TIME

4 ▶ Write Interview Questions

Have partners move to sit together at desks. Ask them to open their notebooks to the next blank page and spend 5–10 minutes writing questions to ask each other. Walk around and observe them. When most students have written at least three questions, signal for their attention.

5 ▶ Interview and Write About Their Partner

Explain that partners will interview each other and then write answers to their questions. Remind them to ask each other follow-up questions to get more information.

Have partners talk and write quietly for 15–20 minutes. Walk around and observe.

Teacher Note

If you notice students having difficulty writing questions, support them by asking them questions such as:

Q *What can you ask your partner about his or her family?*

Q *What can you ask your partner about his or her likes and dislikes?*

Q *What else can you ask your partner about his or her life in or out of school?*

CLASS ASSESSMENT NOTE

Observe the students and ask yourself:

* Were the students able to write questions to ask their partner?

* Do they ask follow-up questions to get more information?

* Do they help each other write answers when needed?

* Are they talking respectfully to each other?

Support struggling pairs by having one partner ask the other a question, listening to the answer, and asking:

Q *What can you write to capture what your partner just said?*

Q *What else can you ask your partner about [what she likes to do on the weekend]?*

Record your observations in the *Assessment Resource Book*.

Signal to let the students know when writing time is over.

SHARING AND REFLECTING

 ## Share About Their Partner

Ask the students to review the questions and answers they wrote about their partner and to pick one to share with the class. Encourage them to pick a question and answer that gives interesting information about their partner.

After allowing a few moments for the students to select their questions and answers, go around the room and have the students read their questions and answers aloud. When all of the students have shared, ask and briefly discuss:

Q *What is something you learned about another student that you didn't know before?*

Q *What question do you want to ask a classmate about what you heard?*

Point out that asking questions of other students helps them get to know one another and build the writing community. Explain that questioning is an important skill for any writer, especially a nonfiction writer, and that they will have further opportunities to practice asking questions in the coming days.

EXTENSION

Learn More About and Write to Koko

Have the students visit www.koko.org to learn more about Koko and gorillas. At this site, you can sign up to receive free online teaching materials, as well as e-mail from Penny and Koko. The students might also send questions by e-mail to kids@koko.org or by mail to KIDS, The Gorilla Foundation, P.O. Box 620530, Woodside, CA 94062.

Day 4

Materials

- *How to Be a Friend*
- *Koko's Kitten*

Exploring Nonfiction

In this lesson, the students:

- Hear and discuss nonfiction
- Discuss a table of contents
- Write about how to be a friend
- Draw illustrations that correspond or add to their writing
- Express interest in and appreciation for one another's writing

GETTING READY TO WRITE

1 Read *How to Be a Friend* Aloud

Gather the class with partners sitting together, facing you. Show the cover of *Koko's Kitten* and remind the students that they learned about a special friendship in this book. Ask and briefly discuss:

Q *What special friendships did you learn about in* Koko's Kitten? *What did you learn about those friendships?*

Explain that today the students will hear another nonfiction book about friendship. Show the title page of *How to Be a Friend* and read the title, subtitle, and authors' names aloud. Show page 3, "Contents," and explain that nonfiction books often have a table of contents, a page that lists the topics in the book and the page numbers where the information about each topic starts. Read the table of contents aloud. Explain that you will read about a few of these topics today.

Read pages 12–15 and 20–32 aloud, showing the illustrations and reading the thought and speech bubbles.

Teacher Note

Several friendships are discussed in this book, including the ones between Koko and Dr. Patterson, Koko and All Ball, and Koko and Lipstick. The book even mentions kittens who had been abandoned by their mother and raised by a dog.

Teacher Note

To provide more time for writing today, we suggest reading only parts of the book aloud. If your writing time and the interest of your students allow, read more of the book. Otherwise, consider making the book available for the students to read on their own after the lesson.

ELL Vocabulary

English Language Learners may benefit from discussing the following vocabulary:

deaf: unable to hear (p. 13)

compliment: say something nice to (p. 15)

are getting divorced: will no longer be married to each other (p. 15)

ignore: pay no attention to (p. 21)

Ask and briefly discuss:

Q *What is something you learned from this nonfiction book?*

Q *How is this nonfiction book the same as or different from Koko's Kitten?*

Students might say:

"*Koko's Kitten* tells a true story, but *How to Be a Friend* doesn't tell a story."

"Both books give information."

"*How to Be a Friend* tells how to do something. *Koko's Kitten* doesn't. It tells *about* something."

2 ▶ Discuss the Use of Illustrations

Point out that although the illustrations make *How to Be a Friend* look like fiction, this is a nonfiction book with true information about how to be a friend. Show and reread pages 30–31 aloud, and then ask:

Q *How do the illustrations help the reader understand the writing?*

Students might say:

"They show in pictures what the authors say in words."

"They give ideas about how to do something the authors say to do."

"They give words you can use when talking to a friend."

Think Before Writing

Explain that today the students will write their own nonfiction pieces about how to be a friend. Before they begin writing, ask them to close their eyes and think about the questions that follow. Ask the questions one at a time (without discussing them), pausing between each one to allow time for the students to think.

Q *Imagine that a new student has come to our class today. What could you do to make friends?*

Q *How could you be a friend to the new student on the playground?*

Q *How could you be a friend at lunch?*

Have the students open their eyes and discuss with their partner their thinking about how to be a friend to a new student. After a few moments, signal for their attention.

WRITING TIME

 Write About Being a Friend

Explain that today the students will write about how to be a friend to someone who is new to the class; then they will add illustrations to their writing. Remind them to use the word wall to help them spell common words and to sound out other unfamiliar words.

Have the students return to their seats and begin writing. Give them about 5 minutes to settle into their writing, and then signal the start of silent writing time. Have them write silently for 20–30 minutes. Join them in writing for a few minutes, and then walk around and observe.

Signal to let the students know when writing time is over.

 ELL Note

English Language Learners may benefit from drawing their ideas before they write. If necessary, write key words and phrases for them to copy.

SHARING AND REFLECTING

5 ▶ Share with a Partner

Gather the class with partners sitting together. Have partners take turns reading their nonfiction pieces and showing their illustrations to each other. Ask:

 Q *How do your partner's illustrations help you understand his or her writing? Turn and tell your partner.*

6 ▶ Discuss Friendship

Point out that the students have thought of a number of ways to be a friend to a new student. Ask and briefly discuss:

Q *Why is it important that we treat everyone in our class as a friend?*

Explain that next week the students will hear and write about a new nonfiction topic.

EXTENSION

Make a Class "How to Be a Friend" Book

You might collect the students' nonfiction pieces about how to be a friend in a class book to place in the classroom library. Periodically revisit the book as a class to remind the students of the different ways they can act like a friend.

Answers to Kids' Frequently Asked Questions About Koko

excerpted from www.koko.org/kidsclub/ask

Is Koko still alive?
Koko is very much alive!

How old is Koko now?
Koko was born on the 4th of July, 1971.

Where does Koko live?
Koko lives at The Gorilla Foundation in Woodside, California, which is in the Santa Cruz Mountains about 35 miles south of San Francisco. She has her own specially equipped trailer and two outdoor play areas.

How does Koko sleep?
Koko, like all gorillas, builds a nest each night to sleep in. Unlike most gorillas, Koko's nest is made out of warm, soft blankets. She usually brings her stuffed dolls to bed with her. She sleeps for about 10 to 13 hours each night.

What do gorillas eat?
Gorillas eat mostly plant foods like leaves, shoots, fruit, bulbs, bark, vines and nettles. They also eat ants, termites, grubs, worms and insect larvae.

What does Koko like to eat?
Koko's diet includes a wide variety of fresh, organic fruits and vegetables. Her favorites are nuts, apples, gourmet tofu dishes and corn on the cob.

Does Koko have a new kitten?
After "All Ball" died in 1984 (as written about in *Koko's Kitten*), Koko was very sad. Koko got a new yellow cat that she named "Lipstick." Following Lipstick's death, Koko got a smoke-gray tailless cat that she named "Smoky." Smoky stayed with Koko for many years, until she passed away of natural causes (at a ripe old age for cats) in 2004.... In 2000, Koko made friends with a black

continues

Answers to Kids' Frequently Asked Questions About Koko

continued

and white kitten named Mo-Mo, who was adopted from the local Humane Society…. Koko was very gentle with all of her cat friends. She cared for her kittens as she would her own tiny gorilla baby, cradling them gently in her arms and carrying them on her back. She has never harmed them, even when they scratch or bite, as kittens sometimes do.

However, today Koko is more interested in having a baby than another kitten.

Does Koko think of Penny as her mother or her sister?

Penny's relationship with Koko is like that of a mother and a daughter. Penny has been with Koko since she was a baby and spends time with her every day. Penny makes sure that Koko is cared for. She feeds Koko, brushes her teeth, reads to her, teaches her and helps get her ready for bed at night.

How does Penny teach Koko?

Penny teaches Koko sign language by making the signs herself while saying the words, and also actually molding Koko's hands into the shape of the signs. Penny goes over vocabulary lists, plays games, gives Koko rewards for right answers to questions, and even gives Koko tests.

UNIT 4: NONFICTION

Paper
by Chris Oxlade
(Heinemann, 2001)

This book takes a close look at paper—its characteristics, how it is made, and how it is used.

Writing Focus

- Students hear, read, and discuss nonfiction.

- Students explore features of a nonfiction book.

- Students write observations, facts, and questions.

Social Focus

- Students make decisions and solve problems respectfully.

- Students build on one another's thinking.

DO AHEAD

- Prior to Day 1, collect one sheet of lined writing paper and one sheet of construction paper for each pair. Also collect multiple sheets of various types of paper (for example, tissue paper, newspaper, cardstock, wrapping paper, wax paper), enough sheets so each pair can have samples of two or three types of paper (a 4" x 5" sheet is a sufficient sample size).

- Prior to Day 3, write the three discussion prompts ("I agree with _____ because…," "I disagree with _____ because…," and "In addition to what _____ said, I think…") on a sheet of chart paper (see the diagram on page 338).

- Prior to Day 3, try the "Which Is Stronger?" experiment (see page 348) to see how it works.

- Prior to Day 4, try the "Suck It Up!" experiment (see page 349) to see how it works.

TEACHER AS WRITER

"The importance of a writer… is that he is here to describe things which other people are too busy to describe."
— James Baldwin

Select an object in the classroom, look at it closely, and write a factual description of it. Provide as much detail as you can about the object's size, shape, color, and other physical attributes.

Day 1

Materials

- *Koko's Kitten* from Week 1
- Sheet of lined writing paper for each pair (see "Do Ahead" on page 327)
- Lined chart paper and a marker
- Sheet of construction paper for each pair (see "Do Ahead" on page 327)
- Multiple sheets of various kinds of paper (see "Do Ahead" on page 327)

Teacher Note ▶

If necessary, remind the students that to *document* something means to *write about it*.

Exploring Nonfiction

In this lesson, the students:

- Observe paper using their senses
- Write observations about paper in pairs
- Play a game using their written observations
- Handle materials responsibly
- Share materials fairly
- Reach agreement before making decisions

GETTING READY TO WRITE

▶ 1 Discuss the Role of Observation in Nonfiction

Have partners sit together at desks today. Show the cover of *Koko's Kitten* and remind the students that they heard and wrote about Koko the gorilla last week. Remind them that Dr. Francine Patterson, the person who taught Koko sign language and wrote the book, observed Koko very closely for many years in order to learn and write about her.

Reread the following passage from the preface to *Koko's Kitten*:

> **p. 5** "Over the years, I have watched Koko grow up. As a scientist, I have documented every phase of her development."

Point out that authors of nonfiction often do research about topics and look closely at things (or *observe* them) in order to learn and write about them. Tell the students that this week they will practice observing something closely and writing nonfiction about it.

▶ 2 Model Writing Observations About Paper

Distribute a blank sheet of lined writing paper to each pair. Explain that before they write on the paper today, the students will look at it very carefully and think about how to describe it. Use "Think, Pair, Share" to have partners first think about and then discuss:

 Q   *What are some ways to describe your sheet of paper?* [pause]
Turn to your partner.

After a few moments, signal for the students' attention and have a few volunteers share their ideas with the class. Title a sheet of lined chart paper "Descriptions of Paper." Underneath the title, write the subheading *Lined writing paper* and record the students' ideas as simple sentences.

Descriptions of Paper

Lined writing paper

*   It is smooth. It is white. It is a flat rectangle with*

rounded corners. There are three holes on one side.

It has blue lines on both sides. It is very thin.

Distribute one sheet of construction paper to each pair, and repeat this procedure. Encourage the students to use different senses to explore their paper, including sight, touch, sound (they might crumple their paper), and smell. After pairs have explored their construction paper, have volunteers share their observations. Record them on the "Descriptions of Paper" chart under the subheading *Construction paper*.

Descriptions of Paper

Lined writing paper

    It is smooth. It is white. It is a flat rectangle with rounded corners. There are three holes on one side. It has blue lines on both sides. It is very thin.

Construction paper

    It is rough. It is colored. It is a flat rectangle. It is bigger than a sheet of writing paper. It has a special smell. It goes "crunch" when you crumple it.

Reread the two descriptions written on the chart. Point out that these are nonfiction descriptions of two different types of paper.

Explain that pairs will now repeat the process on their own with other types of paper. Show and name each type of paper you have collected (such as tissue paper, newspaper, cardstock, wrapping paper, and wax paper), and write the names of the types of paper on the board. Explain that each pair will receive samples of two or three types of paper to study. Partners will closely observe their samples and together write a description of each sample on the sheet of lined paper. Explain that partners will agree on what to write and share the work.

WRITING TIME

3 ▶ Observe and Write Descriptions of Paper

Distribute two or three paper samples to each pair. Have partners write descriptions for 15–20 minutes. To start, walk around and observe without intervening. If after 5 minutes you notice a pair still having difficulty writing descriptions, ask the partners questions such as:

Q *Look at this type of paper. What color is it? Is it shiny or dull? What other words describe what it looks like? How can you write that as a sentence?*

Q *What words describe how this type of paper feels? How can you write that as a sentence?*

Signal to let the students know when writing time is over.

SHARING AND REFLECTING

4 ▶ Reflect on Working Responsibly

Ask and briefly discuss:

Q *What did you do to make sure you both agreed on what to write?*

Q *What did you and your partner do today to handle and share the paper responsibly?*

Q *If you had problems handling or sharing the paper, what will you do next time to make the work go more smoothly? Why is that important?*

5 ▶ Play "Guess the Paper"

Collect the paper samples and display one sheet of each type where everyone can see it (for example, by tacking the sheets to a bulletin board). Explain that the students will play a guessing game using their descriptions as clues. Model the game by asking a pair to choose one of its descriptions and read the first two or three sentences aloud.

◀ **Teacher Note**

If after 5 minutes you notice that most of the pairs are having difficulty, signal for the class's attention and have a pair share some observations for one type of paper. Ask other pairs with that same type of paper to look at it, feel it, and suggest additional observations. Then have partners resume their work of observing and writing descriptions. Note that it is not a problem if pairs do not finish describing all of their samples, as they will only need one description for the "Guess the Paper" activity in Step 5.

◀ **Teacher Note**

To make it easier for the students to identify the different types of paper, you might number or letter each of the displayed pieces.

Ask the class:

 Q *Which type of paper is this pair describing? Turn to your partner.*

After partners have talked for a moment, signal for their attention. Have a volunteer guess the type of paper. If the guess is incorrect, have another volunteer guess. If necessary, have the pair who wrote the description read additional sentences until a correct guess is given.

Give pairs a moment to decide which description they will read aloud, and then repeat the above process with each pair. If necessary, point out that multiple pairs might describe the same type of paper, but each pair will describe the paper in their own way. Continue playing until all of the pairs have read their descriptions (or, if necessary, plan another time to finish playing the game).

Collect the paper samples and have partners put the lined paper with their descriptions into one of their writing folders.

Day 2

Exploring Nonfiction

Materials
- *Paper*
- Paper towel for each pair
- Chart paper and a marker

In this lesson, the students:

- Discuss a table of contents and a glossary
- Hear and discuss nonfiction
- Write facts and questions about paper as a class
- Write about how paper is used in the classroom
- Get ideas by listening to one another

GETTING READY TO WRITE

1 Explore Book Features and Read *Paper* Aloud

Gather the class with partners sitting together, facing you. Remind them to bring their writing notebooks with them. Review that the students began to explore paper by closely observing and writing descriptions of different kinds of paper. Ask and briefly discuss:

Q *What are some things you've found out about paper so far?*

Show the cover and the title page of *Paper* and read the title and the name of the author aloud. Explain that today the students will learn more about paper by listening to a nonfiction book about it.

Show and review the "Contents" page in *Paper* and read a few of the chapter headings aloud. Then show the "Glossary" on page 30, and explain that it gives definitions for some of the words in the text and that you will use it as you read today. Read pages 4–8 aloud, showing the photographs and stopping to read definitions in the glossary for the words in bold, as necessary.

◀ **Teacher Note**

The purpose of referring to the glossary to define words is to help the students understand its use. To avoid interrupting the flow too much when reading, refer to it only for words in bold that you think the students will need help understanding.

Stop after:

    p. 8   "Other types of paper feel rough when you touch them."

Distribute a paper towel to each pair. Have partners feel and discuss the surface of the paper towel, and compare it to the surface of a page in their writing notebooks.

After a few moments, signal for the students' attention and briefly discuss:

Q *What words could you use to describe the feel of the paper towel? The feel of your notebook page?*

Ask the students to put their paper towels and writing notebooks aside. Reread page 8 aloud and continue reading to page 12. Stop after:

> **p. 12**   "The wood comes from trees."

Have partners carefully tear off a corner of their paper towel and observe and discuss the tear. After a few moments, signal for their attention and briefly discuss:

Q *What do you notice about the paper towel where you tore it?*

> **Students might say:**
>
> "It looks fuzzy."
>
> "You can see the fibers."
>
> "The fibers are soft."

Ask the students to put their paper towels and writing notebooks aside. Reread page 12 aloud and continue reading to the end of page 27.

2▶ **Write Facts About Paper as a Class**

Ask:

 Q *What did you learn about paper from this nonfiction book? Turn to your partner.*

Signal for the students' attention and have several volunteers share with the class. Record their ideas on a sheet of chart paper entitled "Facts About Paper."

Teacher Note

If the students have difficulty generating facts, suggest one or two ideas like those in the diagram and then ask the students to generate more ideas. ▶

> ### Facts About Paper
>
> Paper is used to make lots of things.
>
> It is easy to tear, but also strong.
>
> Some paper feels smooth and some feels rough.
>
> Some paper is absorbent.
>
> Paper is made from tiny fibers.
>
> Millions of trees are cut down to make paper.

Explain that you will continue to add to the "Facts About Paper" chart as the students learn more about paper in the coming days.

Discuss How Paper Is Used in the Classroom

Show and reread page 5 of *Paper*. Ask and briefly discuss:

Q *Look around the room. What are some ways we use paper in our classroom?*

Students might say:

"We use paper to draw and write on."

"Paper is used to make the box for our reading folders."

"We use paper to decorate our bulletin boards."

"The tissue we use to blow our noses is a kind of paper."

Explain that today the students will observe their classroom closely to notice different ways paper is used, and then they will write what they observe in their notebooks. Explain that partners may talk softly with each other to share ideas.

WRITING TIME

4 ▶ Write About Paper in the Classroom

Teacher Note ▶

If you notice individual students struggling to write, ask them questions such as:

Q *Look at this corner of the room. What do you see that is made of paper? What type of paper is it? What do we use it for?*

Have partners move to sit together at desks and begin talking and writing about their observations. Have them work together for 15–20 minutes as you walk around and observe.

Signal to let the students know when writing time is over.

SHARING AND REFLECTING

5 ▶ Reflect on Getting Ideas from Others

Ask and briefly discuss:

Q *What ideas did you get from your partner today?*

6 ▶ Discuss and List Questions

Remind the students that learning about a topic often causes us to have more questions about it. Ask:

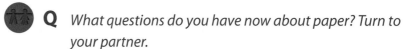 **Q** *What questions do you have now about paper? Turn to your partner.*

After a few moments, signal for the students' attention. Have several volunteers share their questions, and list them on a chart entitled "Questions About Paper."

Questions About Paper

Is paper made from anything else besides wood?

What happens to paper after you throw it away?

Why does paper burn?

Why can you see through some paper?

Do we recycle paper at our school?

Explain that the students will find out more about paper in the coming days.

EXTENSION

Read More Parts of *Paper* Aloud

Show and read the "Fact File" on page 28 of *Paper*. Direct the students' attention to the "Facts About Paper" chart and discuss:

Q   *What fact did you hear that isn't on our chart?*

Add any new facts to the chart.

Show and read "Can You Believe It?" on page 29. Ask and have partners work together to figure out:

Q   *If it takes an adult three hours to walk nine miles, how many miles does the adult walk in one hour?*

Day 3

Materials

- *Paper*
- Charted discussion prompts (see "Do Ahead" on page 327)
- "Facts About Paper" and "Questions About Paper" charts from Day 2
- *Student Writing Handbook* pages 10–11
- One set of materials for the "Which Is Stronger?" experiment (see page 348)
- Lined chart paper and a marker

Teacher Note

This lesson may require an extended time period.

Exploring Nonfiction

In this lesson, the students:

- Read nonfiction that describes how to do something
- Learn discussion prompts to build on one another's thinking
- Observe an experiment and contribute to shared writing about it
- Write about how paper is used at home

GETTING READY TO WRITE

 Teach Discussion Prompts

Have partners get their notebooks and *Student Writing Handbooks* and sit together at desks today. Point out that in a writing community it is important to listen carefully and contribute ideas during discussions. Direct the students' attention to the charted discussion prompts and read them aloud:

> I agree with _____ because...
>
> I disagree with _____ because...
>
> In addition to what _____ said, I think...

Say the prompts aloud together and explain that you would like the students to use the prompts during discussions to help them build on one another's thinking.

Review that the students have been hearing and writing nonfiction. Discuss the following question, encouraging the students to use the discussion prompts as they respond:

Q *What have you found out so far about nonfiction?*

Students might say:

"Nonfiction is not made-up or imaginary."

"I agree with [Jenna] because nonfiction tells about real things."

"In addition to what [Scott] said, nonfiction helps the reader learn something."

"I agree with [Jamal] because some nonfiction helps you learn about something and some tells you how to do something."

Encourage the students to continue to use the prompts as they talk as a whole class today.

 Introduce the "Which Is Stronger?" Experiment

Show the book *Paper* and explain that you will reread two pages of it and then the students will observe and write about an experiment with paper. Reread pages 6–7, "Strong and Weak," aloud.

Direct the students' attention to the "Facts About Paper" and "Questions About Paper" charts. Ask and briefly discuss:

Q *What facts or questions about paper strength do we have on our charts?*

Explain that the students will watch you do an experiment to find out something about paper strength. Have the students open to *Student Writing Handbook* pages 10–11, "Which Is Stronger?" Explain that this is nonfiction writing that tells how to do something, an experiment. Have the students follow along as you read the steps of the experiment aloud.

 Conduct and Write About the "Which Is Stronger?" Experiment

Ask the students to watch as you follow the steps of the experiment. During Steps 3 and 4 of the experiment, have partners discuss what they think will happen, and then discuss what did happen. At the end of the experiment, ask:

Q *What happened in this experiment? Turn to your partner.*

Teacher Note ▶

Model writing a nonfiction narrative about the experiment, rather than writing the steps of the experiment (see the diagram for an example).

FACILITATION TIP

Continue to **ask facilitative questions** to build accountability and participation during class discussions. Redirect students' comments to the class by asking:

Q *Do you agree or disagree with what [Ricki] just said? Why?*

Q *What can you add to what [Ricki] said?*

Much of the learning in this program relies on creating a dynamic discourse among the students. Facilitative questions teach them that their comments contribute to a class discussion, and that they are responsible for listening to one another and responding.

After a moment, signal for the students' attention and explain that you would like the class's help in writing about the experiment. Title a sheet of lined chart paper "The 'Which Is Stronger?' Experiment." Think aloud about why you did the experiment and about the first few steps of it. Ask the students to watch as you write the first one or two sentences. Ask the students for further suggestions, prompting them with questions such as:

Q *What happened next in our experiment? What sentence could I write to describe that?*

Q *What sentence might make sense after this one?*

Q *What did we find out?*

As you write, model using the word wall, approximating spelling, and using appropriate punctuation.

 The "Which Is Stronger?" Experiment

 We did an experiment to find out whether paper is
stronger flat or folded. First, we put the flat paper across
two cans to make a bridge. We put an eraser on the bridge
and the bridge fell. Next, we put the folded paper across
the cans. When we put the eraser on this bridge, it held! We
found out that paper is stronger folded than it is flat.

Reread the chart together as a class. Point out that you wrote what you wanted to find out, what happened, and what you did find out.

Tell the students that they will observe and write about another experiment tomorrow.

4 ▶ Discuss How Paper Is Used at Home

Remind the students that yesterday they wrote about different ways paper is used in the classroom. Explain that today they will write about different ways they use paper at home. Show and reread pages 24–25 of *Paper*, "Paper in Homes." Ask the students to close their eyes and make pictures in their minds as they listen to following questions:

Q *In your mind, look around your kitchen. What do you see that is made of paper? What do you use it for?*

Q *In your mind, look around your bedroom. What do you see that is made of paper? What do you use it for?*

Have two or three volunteers share their thinking with the class. Remind them to use the discussion prompts as they respond.

> **Students might say:**
>
> "In the kitchen we use paper napkins to wipe our hands when we eat."
>
> "In addition to what [Maria] said, cereal boxes are made of paper."
>
> "I have wallpaper in my bedroom."
>
> "In addition to what [Bruce] said, I have books to read in my bedroom."

WRITING TIME

5 ▶ Write About Paper at Home

Have the students open their writing notebooks to the next blank page and work silently for 10–15 minutes to describe different ways they use paper at home. As they work, walk around and observe.

Signal to let the students know when writing time is over.

Teacher Note

If you notice individual students struggling to write, ask them questions such as:

Q *Close your eyes. In your mind, picture [the room where you watch television]. Look around you. What do you see that is made of paper? What type of paper is it? What do you use it for?*

SHARING AND REFLECTING

6 ▶ Share Writing and Reflect on Learning

Explain that partners will read their writing to each other and talk about things made of paper that they both have in their homes.

After a few minutes, signal for the students' attention. Ask and briefly discuss:

Q *What are some things made of paper that you and your partner both have at home?*

Q (Point to the "Facts About Paper" chart.) *What new facts can we add to our "Facts About Paper" chart?*

Q (Point to the "Questions About Paper" chart.) *What questions can we add to our "Questions About Paper" chart?*

Record the students' suggestions on the charts.

7 ▶ Reflect on Using the Discussion Prompts

Ask and briefly discuss:

Q *How did we do with using the discussion prompts during our class discussion today?*

Q *How do the discussion prompts help us talk as a class?*

Encourage the students to continue to use the discussion prompts whenever they can in class discussions.

Teacher Note

Save the shared writing chart—"The 'Which Is Stronger?' Experiment"—to use on Day 4. Continue to display the charted discussion prompts throughout the unit and until the students use these prompts naturally.

Day 4

Exploring Nonfiction

In this lesson, the students:

- Read nonfiction that describes how to do something
- Observe an experiment and write about it in pairs
- Use discussion prompts to build on one another's thinking
- Reach agreement before making decisions
- Contribute to and include one another in group work

GETTING READY TO WRITE

1 Briefly Review Discussion Prompts

Have partners get their *Student Writing Handbooks* and sit together at desks today. Remind the students that they learned three discussion prompts yesterday to help them connect their ideas with the ideas of others during class discussions. Point to the charted discussion prompts and read them aloud together. Remind the students to use the prompts when they participate in the discussion today.

2 Introduce the "Suck It Up!" Experiment

Review that yesterday the students observed an experiment about paper and contributed to shared writing about it. Briefly review the shared writing chart, "The 'Which Is Stronger?' Experiment."

Explain that today the students will observe another experiment, and then partners will write about it. Ask the students to listen as you reread a few pages of *Paper*. Read pages 10–11 and pages 16–17

Materials

- *Paper*
- "The 'Which Is Stronger?' Experiment" chart from Day 3
- Charted discussion prompts from Day 3
- "Facts About Paper" and "Questions About Paper" charts
- *Student Writing Handbook* page 12–13
- One set of materials for the "Suck It Up!" experiment (see page 349)
- Loose, lined paper
- *Assessment Resource Book*

◀ **Teacher Note**

The discussion prompts are:

- "I agree with _____ because…"
- "I disagree with _____ because…"
- "In addition to what _____ said, I think…"

aloud. Direct the students' attention to the "Facts About Paper" and "Questions About Paper" charts. Ask and briefly discuss:

Q *What facts or questions about paper's absorbency (its ability to soak up liquid) do we have on our charts?*

Have the students open to *Student Writing Handbook* pages 12–13, "Suck It Up!" and follow along as you read the steps of the experiment aloud.

3 ▶ Conduct the "Suck It Up!" Experiment

Ask the students to watch as you follow the steps of the experiment. Stop before each step to have partners discuss what they think will happen. Stop after each step to discuss what did happen. At the end of the experiment, use "Think, Pair, Share" to have partners first think about and then discuss:

Q *What happened in this experiment?* [pause] *Turn to your partner.*

Q *What did you find out about paper from this experiment?* [pause] *Turn to your partner.*

After partners have discussed the experiment, signal for their attention. Explain that partners will work together to write about the experiment, just as the class did yesterday. They may look at yesterday's shared writing chart, "The 'Which Is Stronger?' Experiment," to help them as they write. Remind partners to agree on what to write and to share the work.

WRITING TIME

4 ▶ Write About the "Suck It Up!" Experiment

Distribute a sheet of lined writing paper to each pair and have partners talk and write about the experiment for 10–15 minutes. As they work, walk around and observe.

Teacher Note

If you notice students simply copying the steps of the experiment out of their *Student Writing Handbooks*, have them put their handbooks away before continuing.

CLASS ASSESSMENT NOTE

Observe pairs without intervening for 5 minutes, asking yourself:

- Are pairs able to discuss and agree on sentences to write?

- If they disagree, do they keep talking until they agree?

- Do they write sentences that make sense and describe what happened?

After 5 minutes, if you notice pairs having difficulty writing about the experiment, support them by asking them questions such as:

Q *What did we want to find out by doing this experiment?*

Q *What did we do to find out?*

Q *What did you find out about paper in the experiment? How can you write that as a sentence?*

If you notice most pairs in the class having difficulty after 5 minutes, signal for the students' attention and write the first two or three sentences together as a class, following the procedure you used in Day 3, Step 3 (see pages 339–340). Then have pairs resume writing on their own for a few more minutes.

Record your observations in the *Assessment Resource Book*.

Signal for the students' attention. Have partners reread their writing to make sure they have told what they found out from the experiment and to see what more they might tell. Give them about 5 more minutes to write.

Signal to let the students know when writing time is over.

SHARING AND REFLECTING

5 ▶ Share Writing in Groups of Four

Explain that pairs will now combine to form groups of four to share their writing. One partner in each pair will read the pair's writing aloud as the other pair listens. Give pairs a moment to decide which partner will read the writing aloud to the group; then have pairs combine to form groups of four and begin sharing. Walk around and observe.

After pairs have had time to share their writing, signal for their attention. Ask and have the groups of four discuss:

Q *What was the same about what both pairs wrote? What was different?*

Signal for the students' attention and have several volunteers share their thinking with the class.

6 ▶ Reflect on Sharing in Groups of Four

Ask:

Q *How is talking in a group of four easier or harder than talking with a partner? Talk to the others in your group.*

After a few moments, signal for the students' attention and have a few volunteers share their thinking with the class. If necessary, remind the students to use the discussion prompts.

Point out that the students learned about paper this week by observing it, reading about it, and writing about it. Explain that next week the students will explore another topic as they continue to learn about and write nonfiction.

Teacher Note ▶

Working in groups of four can be more challenging for students than working in pairs. If you notice many students having difficulty either participating or including one another in the group discussion, signal for the class's attention and discuss the following questions:

Q *Why is it important for everyone in the group to participate in the discussion?*

Q *What can you do to make sure you are contributing your ideas to the group?*

Q *What can you do to help if you notice others in the group are not participating?*

Encourage the students to take responsibility by both contributing to and including one another in the group work. Have groups resume their work together for a few more minutes.

EXTENSION

Explore and Write About Recycling

Find out more about recycling efforts, particularly for paper, in your classroom or at your school. Conduct a student walk around the classroom or school to observe these efforts, and then discuss how they might be improved. Develop a recycling plan and write letters to potential participants such as the principal, teachers, students, and parents.

The following books provide recycling information, activities, and resources for students: *Recycle! A Handbook for Kids* by Gail Gibbons, *Recycling* by Rhonda Lucas Donald, *Garbage and Recycling: Environmental Facts and Experiments* by Rosie Harlow and Sally Morgan, *Recycle That!* by Fay Robinson, *Earth Book for Kids: Activities to Help Heal the Environment* by Linda Schwartz, *Where Does the Garbage Go?* by Paul Showers, and *50 Simple Things Kids Can Do to Save the Earth* by the EarthWorks Group.

You might also search online using the keywords "recycling for students." Many websites provide lesson plans for teachers as well as activities and information for students.

Experiment

Which Is Stronger?

Which is stronger, a flat piece of paper or a folded one? Try this experiment to find out.

What You Need:

2 sheets of paper

2 cans that are the same size

Small object that won't break, such as an eraser or marker

What You Do:

1. Fold one sheet of paper "accordion" style by making a ½" fold along the long edge of the paper, turning the sheet over and making another fold the same width as the first fold, and continuing to fold back and forth until the entire sheet is folded. Set this folded piece of paper aside.

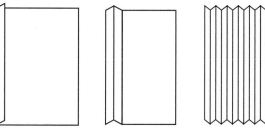

2. Put the two cans in front of you about 5" apart. Place the unfolded sheet of paper on top to make a bridge.

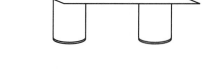

3. Think: If you put your object on the bridge, will it hold or fall? After you guess, try it to see what happens.

4. Do the same experiment with the folded piece of paper. Remember, think first about what you think will happen, and then try it.

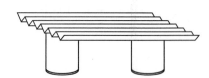

5. What did you find out? Write about your thinking.

Experiment

Suck It Up!

Which is more absorbent, a sheet of paper or a paper towel? Try this experiment to find out.

What You Need:

2 paper towels
2 sheets of writing paper
Marker
Squeeze bottle or a jar with a dropper
Water

What You Do:

1. On a paper towel, drop a little water. Talk about what happens.

2. Drop the same amount of water onto one of the sheets of writing paper. Talk about what happens.

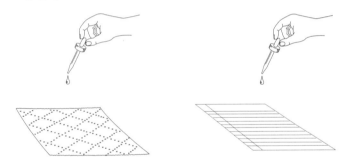

3. On the other paper towel, draw a happy face using a marker. Talk about what you notice.

4. On the other sheet of writing paper, draw a happy face using a marker. Talk about what you notice.

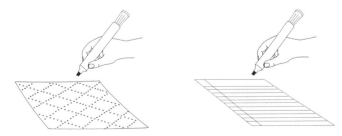

5. Think: Which is more absorbent, the paper towel or the writing paper?

UNIT 4: NONFICTION

Polar Lands
by Margaret Hynes
(Kingfisher, 2007)

This book explores the Arctic and Antarctic—including their natural features and the people and animals who live there.

Writing Focus

- Students hear, read, and discuss nonfiction.

- Students write questions and information about the polar lands.

- Students write about the animals and people of the polar lands.

- Students list topics of interest about the polar lands.

- Students choose a topic about the polar lands and write about it.

Social Focus

- Students build on one another's thinking.

- Students act in fair and caring ways.

- Students listen respectfully to the thinking of others and share their own.

- Students express interest in and appreciation for one another's writing.

DO AHEAD

- Prior to Day 1, consider previewing *Polar Lands* with your English Language Learners. Read it aloud and show and discuss the photographs, or have the students flip through it on their own. (See pages 353, 357, and 361 for suggested ELL vocabulary.)

- Prior to Day 4, choose a topic about the polar lands and prepare to model writing about it (see Day 4, Step 1, on pages 364–365).

TEACHER AS WRITER

"Curiosity urges you on—the driving force."
— *John Dos Passos*

Nonfiction writers aren't necessarily experts on the topics they set out to write about, but they are curious about them. They communicate what they learn about a topic in a way that makes their readers curious, too. List some topics you are curious about. Ask yourself:

- What part of the world do you wish you knew more about?

- What in the natural world have you always wanted to understand?

- What is something you take for granted that you wish you knew more about?

- What current event do you wish you knew the history behind?

Day 1

Materials

- *Polar Lands*
- Charted discussion prompts from Week 2
- Chart paper and a marker

Teacher Note ▶

The discussion prompts are:

- "I agree with _____ because…"
- "I disagree with _____ because…"
- "In addition to what _____ said, I think…"

Exploring Nonfiction

In this lesson, the students:

- Hear and discuss nonfiction
- List information they hear in the reading
- Write questions about the polar lands
- Use discussion prompts to build on one another's thinking
- Get ideas by listening to one another
- Ask for and give help respectfully

GETTING READY TO WRITE

▶1 Briefly Review the Discussion Prompts

Have partners get their writing notebooks and sit together at desks today. Remind the students that they learned three discussion prompts to help them connect their ideas with the ideas of others during class discussions. Point to the charted discussion prompts and read them aloud together. Remind the students to use the prompts when they participate in the class discussion today.

▶2 Read Parts of *Polar Lands* Aloud

Gather the class with partners sitting together, facing you. Remind the students that last week they wrote observations, facts, questions, and nonfiction pieces about paper. Explain that this week they will hear and write about another nonfiction topic.

Show *Polar Lands* and read the title and the author's name aloud. Explain that this nonfiction book tells about the coldest places on earth. Explain that the students will hear parts of *Polar Lands* over the next several days. Today you will read several pages about where the polar lands are located and what they are like. Ask the students to listen for information about the polar lands.

Read pages 6–7 and 10–11 aloud, showing the photographs and discussing the diagrams. Point out that nonfiction text often has illustrations, maps, diagrams, and other graphics that give the reader more information about the topic.

ELL Vocabulary

English Language Learners may benefit from discussing the following vocabulary:

regions: areas (p. 6)

surrounds: is all around (p. 7)

glorious: beautiful (p. 11)

constant daylight: sun always being out, even during the night (p. 11)

◀ **Teacher Note**

At the bottom of nearly every page in this book, there is a definition for one of the words on that page. Since these words are defined on the page, they are not included as suggested vocabulary.

3 ▶ Reread and List More Information

Without discussing the reading, explain that you will reread the pages and ask the students to listen for information about the polar lands that they might have missed during the first reading. Reread pages 6–7 and 10–11 aloud.

Ask and briefly discuss the question that follows. Refer to the charted discussion prompts and remind the students to use the prompts as they respond.

Q *What are some interesting things you learned about the polar lands?*

Students might say:

"I learned that the polar lands are at the North and South Poles."

"I agree with [Leigh] because the Arctic is at the North Pole and Antarctica is at the South Pole."

"In addition to what [Jonathan] said, I learned that the polar lands are the coldest places on earth."

"I agree with [Rodolpho]. Everything is almost always frozen in the polar lands."

As the students respond, list their ideas as brief sentences on a sheet ◀ of chart paper entitled "Interesting Things About the Polar Lands."

Teacher Note

The goal of this activity is for the students to begin to identify information in nonfiction text, rather than to develop a complete list of facts. Gently encourage the students to express the information in their own words. Throughout the week, move the charting activities along quickly to maintain student interest.

> *Interesting Things About the Polar Lands*
>
> The polar lands are at the North and South Poles.
>
> The Arctic is at the North Pole.
>
> The Antarctic is at the South Pole.
>
> They are the coldest places on earth.
>
> Everything is frozen most of the time.
>
> It is dark most of the day in the winter.
>
> The sun stays out for weeks in the summer.

Explain that you will continue to chart information as the students learn more about the polar lands in the coming days.

▶ 4 Think Before Writing

Remind the students that reading nonfiction often leads readers to have more questions about the topic. Use "Think, Pair, Share" to have partners first think about and then discuss:

 Q   *What questions do you have about the polar lands?* [pause] *Turn to your partner.*

After a few moments, signal for the students' attention and have two or three volunteers share a question with the class. If necessary, stop to remind them to use the discussion prompts.

WRITING TIME

▶ 5 Discuss and Write Questions About the Polar Lands

Explain that today the students will write questions they have about the polar lands, and that they may talk softly with their partner to share ideas and to help each other write.

Have partners move to sit together at desks. Have them open to the next blank page in their notebooks and begin discussing and writing their questions about the polar lands. Point out that each student will write her own questions after partners have talked. Have them write for 15–20 minutes.

Join the students in writing for a few minutes, and then walk around and observe.

Signal to let the students know when writing time is over.

SHARING AND REFLECTING

 Reflect on Working with a Partner

Ask and briefly discuss:

Q *During writing time today, what did your partner do that was helpful to you?*

Q *What is an idea that your partner shared with you?*

Explain that tomorrow the students will share the questions they wrote and hear more about the polar lands.

Teacher Note

Save the "Interesting Things About the Polar Lands" chart to use the rest of this week.

Day 2

Materials

- *Polar Lands*
- "Interesting Things About the Polar Lands" chart from Day 1
- *Student Writing Handbook* pages 14–15
- Chart paper and a marker

Exploring Nonfiction

In this lesson, the students:

- Share their questions about the polar lands
- Hear and read about polar animals
- List information they hear in the reading
- Write about sea mammals
- Get ideas by listening to one another
- Ask for and give help respectfully

GETTING READY TO WRITE

 Share Questions About the Polar Lands

Gather the class with partners sitting together, facing you. Have them bring their notebooks and their *Student Writing Handbooks* with them.

Review that yesterday the students heard part of the book *Polar Lands*, listed information they learned, and wrote questions that they have. Briefly review the "Interesting Things About the Polar Lands" chart; then have the students silently review the questions they wrote in their notebooks and each pick one to share with the class.

Go around the class and have each student read a question aloud. Invite the students to listen during the read-aloud today to see if any of their questions are answered.

 Read More of *Polar Lands* Aloud

Explain that you will read information about some of the animals that live in the polar lands. Read pages 18–19 and 28–29 aloud, showing the illustrations and clarifying vocabulary as you read.

Suggested Vocabulary

coastal areas: land along the ocean (p. 28)

ELL Vocabulary

English Language Learners may benefit from discussing additional vocabulary, including:

blubber: thick fat (p. 18)
stray: wander (p. 19)
snuggle: get close and comfortable (p. 29)

 Reread and List Information

Without discussing the reading, explain that you will reread the pages, and ask the students to listen for information they might have missed during the first reading. Reread pages 18–19 and 28–29 aloud. Ask:

Q   *What are some things you learned about animals that live in the polar lands?*

Have a few volunteers share their thinking. List their ideas as brief sentences on a sheet of chart paper entitled "Animals in the Polar Lands." If necessary, stop to remind the students to use the discussion prompts.

4 **Read About Sea Mammals**

Have the students open to *Student Writing Handbook* pages 14–15, where the chapter from *Polar Lands* called "Sea Mammals" is reproduced. Invite them to follow along as you read this section aloud. Read pages 24–25 aloud, clarifying vocabulary as you read.

Suggested Vocabulary

mammals: warm-blooded animals that feed milk to their young (p. 24)
levers: small things that can be pushed down to lift a large weight (p. 25)

Explain that today partners will work together to write information they learned about sea mammals from the reading. Ask them to follow along and listen carefully as you reread these pages aloud. After the second reading, ask:

 Q *What information did you learn about sea mammals? Turn to your partner.*

After a few moments, signal for the students' attention and have a few volunteers share their thinking.

WRITING TIME

 5 **Write About Sea Mammals**

Restate that the students will write interesting things they learned about sea mammals from the reading. Tell them that they may refer back to the reading, and that partners may talk softly to each other to share ideas and to help each other write.

Have partners move to sit together at desks. Have them open to the next blank page in their writing notebooks and begin discussing and writing information they learned about sea mammals. Remind them that each student will do his own writing. Have them write for 15–20 minutes.

Join the students in writing for a few minutes, and then walk around and observe.

Signal to let the students know when writing time is over.

SHARING AND REFLECTING

6 **Reflect on Learning**

Ask and briefly discuss:

 Q *What is something you learned about sea mammals today?*

As volunteers respond, record the information as brief sentences on the "Animals in the Polar Lands" chart.

Explain that tomorrow the students will hear about the people who live in the polar lands.

Teacher Note

Save the "Animals in the Polar Lands" chart to use the rest of this week.

Day 3

Materials

- *Polar Lands*
- Chart paper and a marker
- "Interesting Things About the Polar Lands" chart
- "Animals in the Polar Lands" chart from Day 2

Exploring Nonfiction

In this lesson, the students:

- Hear and discuss nonfiction
- List information they hear in the reading
- List writing topics
- Share their partner's thinking with the class

GETTING READY TO WRITE

 Read More of *Polar Lands* Aloud

Gather the class with partners sitting together, facing you. Have them bring their writing notebooks with them. Remind the students that yesterday they learned about animals in the polar lands.

Ask the students to take a moment to review the questions they wrote in their notebooks about the polar lands. Ask and briefly discuss:

Q *Which questions have you heard information about so far?*

Explain that today you will read from *Polar Lands* about the people who live there. Ask and briefly discuss:

Q *What questions did you write about how people live in the polar lands?*

Invite the students to listen for answers to their questions as you read today. Read pages 30–33 aloud, clarifying vocabulary as you read.

Suggested Vocabulary

traditionally: for a long time, over many generations (p. 30)

2▸ Reread and List Information

Without discussing the reading, explain that you will reread the pages and ask the students to listen for information about the Inuit people and the herders that they might have missed during the first reading. Reread pages 30–33 aloud. Ask:

Q *What are some things you learned about the people who live in the polar lands?*

Have a few volunteers share their thinking. List their ideas as brief sentences on a sheet of chart paper entitled "People in the Polar Lands." If necessary, remind the students to use the discussion prompts.

3▸ Repeat Steps 1 and 2 with Additional Readings

Repeat the procedure you used in Steps 1 and 2 with pages 36–37 and 40–41 of *Polar Lands*: read the pages aloud, reread, and list information.

Suggested Vocabulary

processed: taken through several steps to make into usable fuel (p. 37)

endangered: put in danger of becoming extinct, or of not existing anymore (p. 40)

ELL Vocabulary

English Language Learners may benefit from discussing additional vocabulary, including:

improvements: changes that make something better (p. 36)

distributed: delivered (p. 36)

harming: hurting (p. 40)

environment: land, plants, and animals around us (p. 40)

airlifted: taken by plane or helicopter (p. 40)

tourists: sightseers (p. 41)

4▸ Generate Topics of Interest

Remind the students that they learned many things about the polar lands this week. Refer to the charts from Days 1 and 2 and the chart from today; briefly review the information about the polar lands and the people and animals that live there. Explain that tomorrow the students will write a nonfiction piece about something they think is interesting about the polar lands.

Use "Think, Pair Share" to have partners first think about and then discuss:

 Q *What do you find interesting about the polar lands that you might like to write about?* [pause] *Turn to your partner.*

After a minute or two, signal for the students' attention and have a few volunteers share their thinking. Explain that today the students will list at least three things about the polar lands that they might like to write about tomorrow.

WRITING TIME

▶5 List Possible Writing Topics

Have the students return to their seats and work silently for 10 minutes to list in their notebooks at least three things about the polar lands that they might like to write about.

Join the students in writing for a few minutes, and then walk around and observe.

Signal to let the students know when writing time is over.

Teacher Note ▶

If you notice a student is struggling to list ideas, you might direct her attention to the charts about the polar lands and ask her if she was more interested in the people, the animals, or the land. You might also share topics of interest to you. You might say, "I thought hearing about how the polar bear is the 'king of the ice' was very interesting. I'd like to write about polar bears. What do you find interesting that you would like to write about?"

SHARING AND REFLECTING

▶6 Share Writing Topics

Gather the class with partners sitting together, facing you. Explain that partners will read their lists of possible writing topics to each other. Alert the students to listen carefully, as they will share their partner's ideas with the class. Have partners read their lists of topics to each other. Ask and briefly discuss:

 Q *What is something your partner might write about tomorrow?*

Teacher Note

Save the "People in the Polar Lands" chart to use on Day 4.

Explain that the students have not heard all of *Polar Lands* and that you will put the book in the classroom library for them to read on their own, if they wish.

EXTENSION

Learn More About the Polar Lands

You might read aloud the pages of *Polar Lands* that you have not yet read to the class (pages 8–9, 12–17, 20–23, 26–27, 34–35, and 38–39) to provide the students with more information about their questions. You might also have the students identify and use other sources of information, including library books, the encyclopedia, and the Internet. Some useful books include: *Life in the Polar Lands* by Monica Byles, *Polar Lands* by Claire Watts, *Arctic Tundra* by Michael H. Forman, *Amazing Arctic Animals* by Jackie Glassman, and *This Place is Cold* by Vicki Cobb.

Day 4

Materials

- Lined chart paper and a marker
- "Interesting Things About the Polar Lands" chart
- "Animals in the Polar Lands" chart
- "People in the Polar Lands" chart from Day 3
- *Assessment Resource Book*

Exploring Nonfiction

In this lesson, the students:

- Choose topics
- Write about the polar lands
- Express interest in and appreciation for one another's writing
- Ask one another questions about their writing

GETTING READY TO WRITE

 Model Writing About a Topic

Gather the class with partners sitting together, facing you. Have them bring their writing notebooks with them. Review that yesterday the students listed at least three interesting topics about the polar lands that they might like to write about. Today they will pick one of these topics and write some nonfiction about it.

Ask the students to watch as you model beginning to write about the topic you have chosen (see "Do Ahead" on page 351). Think aloud and write the first one or two sentences of a piece about the topic (see the diagram). Ask the students for suggestions as you continue to write the piece, prompting them with questions such as:

Q *What sentence shall I write next?*

Q *What else can we write about [polar bears]?*

Q *What other information on our chart could we write about?*

Q *What sentence might make sense after this one?*

As you write, model using the ▶ word wall, approximating spelling, and using appropriate punctuation.

> _Polar bears are the largest, most powerful land_
>
> _animals of the Arctic. They are strong swimmers and can_
>
> _hunt seals on the ice floes and in the water. Their oily fur_
>
> _and blubber keep them warm as they hunt. Polar bears have_
>
> _sharp claws that they use to catch fish._

Reread the piece together as a class.

2 ▶ Choose Writing Topics

Have the students look at the list of topics they wrote yesterday
and each choose one topic to write about that is different from
the shared writing topic. Have partners tell each other their topics
and discuss:

 Q *What information might you include in your piece? Turn to
your partner.*

After a few minutes, signal for the students' attention.

WRITING TIME

3 ▶ Write About the Polar Lands

Explain that today the students will write silently about their topics.
Remind them to use the word wall to help them spell common
words and to sound out other words. Encourage them to use the
information on the charts to help them write.

Have the students return to their seats and write silently for 20–30 minutes. Join them in writing for a few minutes, and then walk around and observe.

CLASS ASSESSMENT NOTE

Observe the students and ask yourself:

- Are the students excited to write about their topics?

- Do they include factual information?

- Do they use the charts from earlier in the week to help them write?

Support the students by asking questions such as:

Q *What topic have you chosen? What do you want to tell about this topic?*

Q *How might you write this information in a way makes others interested in it, too? What might you say first?*

Q *What is something else you might tell? How might you say that in your own words?*

Record your observations in the *Assessment Resource Book*.

Signal to let the students know when writing time is over.

SHARING AND REFLECTING

 Share Interesting Sentences

Ask the students to read their nonfiction pieces quietly to themselves and each choose one interesting sentence to share with the class. After a few moments, signal for their attention. Go around the room and, without comment, have the students share their sentences. When all of the students have shared, ask and briefly discuss:

Q *What sentence did you hear that you found interesting? Why did that sentence grab your attention?*

Q *What question do you want to ask [Flor] about the sentence [she] wrote?*

Explain that next week the students will continue to hear and write nonfiction.

EXTENSION

Explore Activities in *Polar Lands*

Have the students do one or more of the activities on pages 42–47 in *Polar Lands*. Point out that the written activities are examples of *functional writing*, a kind of nonfiction that tells how to do something. Ask:

Q *What do you notice about how this "how to" nonfiction is written?*

> **Students might say:**
>
> "It tells you what to do."
>
> "I agree with [Nani] because it gives you steps for the project."
>
> "In addition to what [Billy] said, it tells you what materials you need."

Week 4 Overview

UNIT 4: NONFICTION

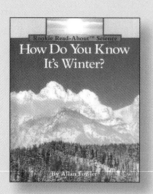

How Do You Know It's Winter?
by Allan Fowler
(Childrens Press, 1991)

This book describes the many ways to tell that it is winter.

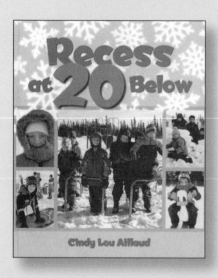

Recess at 20 Below
by Cindy Lou Aillaud
(Alaska Northwest Books, 2006)

Even when it's 20 below, students in Alaska go out to recess.

Writing Focus

- Students hear and discuss nonfiction.

- Students write about seasons where they live.

- Students select drafts to publish.

- Students reread and add descriptive language.

- Students confer with one another and the teacher.

Social Focus

- Students build on one another's thinking.

- Students act in fair and caring ways.

- Students help one another improve their writing.

- Students express interest in and appreciation for one another's writing.

DO AHEAD

- Prior to Day 2, consider previewing *Recess at 20 Below* with your English Language Learners. Read it aloud and show and discuss the photographs, or have the students flip through it on their own. (See page 375 for suggested ELL vocabulary.)

- Prior to Day 2, prepare a small card for each pair with one of the following seasons written on it: *spring*, *summer*, or *fall*. Try to make about the same number of cards for each season. Fold the cards and place them in a paper bag.

TEACHER AS WRITER

"We write about what we don't know about what we know."
— *Grace Paley*

Choose one of the topics you listed last week and write that topic at the top of a blank page in your notebook. Write five questions you have about the topic. Choose one to research and write about.

Day 1

Materials

- *How Do You Know It's Winter?*
- Charted discussion prompts from Week 2

Teacher Note

The discussion prompts are:

- "I agree with _____ because…"
- "I disagree with _____ because…"
- "In addition to what _____ said, I think…"

Exploring Nonfiction

In this lesson, the students:

- Hear and discuss nonfiction
- Write about winter where they live
- Use discussion prompts to build on one another's thinking
- Get ideas by listening to one another
- Express interest in one another's writing
- Ask one another questions about their writing

GETTING READY TO WRITE

▶ 1 Briefly Review the Discussion Prompts

Gather the class with partners sitting together, facing you. Remind the students that they learned three discussion prompts to help them connect their ideas with the ideas of others during class discussions. Point to the charted discussion prompts and read them aloud together. Ask and briefly discuss:

Q *How does using the discussion prompts help us during discussions?*

Students might say:

"The prompts help us listen to what people say."

"I agree with [Zoe] because you have to listen if you are going to agree or disagree with someone."

"In addition to what [Russell] said, hearing different people's ideas helps us learn."

Encourage the students to use the prompts when they participate in the discussion today.

2 Read *How Do You Know It's Winter?* Aloud

Review that last week the students heard a nonfiction book about the coldest places on earth. Explain that today they will hear a nonfiction book about the coldest season of the year, winter. Show the cover of *How Do You Know It's Winter?* and read the title and the author's name aloud. Ask and briefly discuss:

Q *What time of year is winter?*

Q *What do you think are some things Allan Fowler might tell us about winter?*

Teacher Note

You might refer to the classroom calendar to identify the winter months where you live.

Invite the students to listen to what the author has to say about winter. Read the book aloud, showing the photographs as you read.

ELL Vocabulary

English Language Learners may benefit from discussing the following vocabulary:

bundle up: put on lots of warm clothes (p. 14)

Ask and briefly discuss:

Q *What does the author tell us about winter?*

3 Discuss Winter Where They Live

Use "Think, Pair, Share" to have partners first think about and then discuss:

Q *If you wanted to write about what winter is like where we live, what might you write?* [pause] *Turn to your partner.*

After a moment, signal for the students' attention and have a few volunteers share their thinking with the class. As the students share, ask follow-up questions such as:

Q *What are some of the things you like to do with your family during winter?*

ELL Note

If necessary, simplify this question by rephrasing it in the following way:

Q *Winter is [snowy] where we live. What else do you know about winter where we live? How could you write that as a sentence?*

FACILITATION TIP

Continue to practice **asking facilitative questions** during class discussions to help the students respond directly to one another. Encourage the students to use the discussion prompts when they respond to one another.

Q *[Wendy] said [the trees don't have leaves]. How might you describe what the [trees] look like to someone who has never been here in the winter?*

Q *[Sammi] said [it snows a lot]. How might you describe a [snowy] day?*

Q *[LaTisha] said [she likes to go ice skating on the pond]. What else do you like to do outside in the winter?*

Explain that today the students will write about what winter is like where they live.

WRITING TIME

4 ▶ Write About Winter

Have the students return to their seats and write for 20–30 minutes about winter where they live. Join the students in writing for a few minutes. When the students are settled into their writing, begin conferring with individual students.

TEACHER CONFERENCE NOTE

During the next two weeks, confer with individual students about their nonfiction writing. Ask each student to read his piece aloud to you as you ask yourself:

- Can I tell what the topic is?

- Is the student writing factual information about the topic?

- Is the writing clear? Does it make sense?

Support students by reading their writing back to them and asking them questions such as:

Q *Does the writing make sense? What do you need to change so it makes sense?*

continues

> **TEACHER CONFERENCE NOTE** *continued*
>
> **Q**   *What more can you tell about [what you do on snow days]?*
>
> Document your observations for each student using the "Conference Notes" record sheet (BLM1).

Signal to let the students know when writing time is over.

SHARING AND REFLECTING

5▶ Share Sentences and Reflect

Ask the students to quietly read their writing and each underline a sentence to share with the class that tells something about winter where they live. After allowing time for them to choose their sentences, go around the room and have each student read her underlined sentence aloud, without comment.

Ask and briefly discuss:

Q   *What did you hear that got you interested in someone else's writing?*

Q   *What questions do you want to ask [Dara] about what [she] wrote?*

Explain that tomorrow the students will hear another nonfiction book about winter.

Day 2

Materials

- *Recess at 20 Below*
- World map
- Paper bag with season cards (see "Do Ahead" on page 369)

Exploring Nonfiction

In this lesson, the students:

- Hear and discuss nonfiction
- Write about spring, summer, or fall where they live
- Express interest in one another's writing
- Ask one another questions about their writing

GETTING READY TO WRITE

 Read *Recess at 20 Below* Aloud

Gather the class with partners sitting together, facing you. Remind the students that they heard *How Do You Know It's Winter?* and thought about what winter is like where they live. Explain that today you will read another nonfiction book about winter.

Show the cover of *Recess at 20 Below* and read the title and the author's name aloud. Explain that this is a true story about recess time in winter for students who live in Alaska. On the world map, locate Alaska in relation to the Arctic and to where you live. Show the title page and explain that "20 Below" means 20 degrees below zero (Fahrenheit) on the thermometer. Contrast that temperature with the temperature outside your classroom today.

Read *Recess at 20 Below* aloud, showing the photographs and clarifying vocabulary as you read.

> **Suggested Vocabulary**
>
> **ravens:** large birds that are similar to crows (p. 23)
> **static:** electrical charge (p. 29)

ELL Vocabulary

English Language Learners may benefit from discussing additional vocabulary, including:

ice crystals: little pieces of ice and snow (p. 5)

maintenance man: person who cleans and takes care of the school (p. 13)

glacier: large area of packed ice and snow (p. 14)

moisture: warm, wet air (p. 21)

pitch-black dark: very, very dark (p. 25)

Ask:

Q *What did you find out about what recess is like in Alaska in the wintertime?*

Q *What makes this book nonfiction?*

Have a few volunteers share their thinking with the class. Remind the students to use the discussion prompts to respond to one another.

2 Generate Ideas About Other Seasons

Remind the students that yesterday they wrote about what winter is like where they live. Explain that today they will write about one of the other seasons. Ask and briefly discuss:

Q *What are the other seasons of the year?*

Q *What months of the year are in the [spring/summer/fall]?*

Q *What is your favorite season? Why?*

Show the bag of cards and explain that each card in the bag has the name of a season written on it. Each pair will pick a card and write about that season today. Walk the bag around and have one partner from each pair select a card and the other partner read it aloud.

When all of the pairs have selected a season to write about, ask the students close their eyes and make pictures in their minds as they listen to the questions that follow. Ask the questions one at a time (without discussing them), pausing between each question to give the students time to visualize.

Q *Think about what your season is like where we live. What is the weather like? What types of clothes do people wear?*

Q *What happens during your season to the trees and plants where we live?*

Q *What happens to the animals and birds?*

Q *What holidays are in your season?*

Q *Do you go to school during your season? If so, does your season come at the beginning, middle, or end of the school year?*

Ask the students to open their eyes and talk with their partner about their season. After a few minutes, signal for the students' attention and ask:

Q *What are some of the things you and your partner discussed about your season?*

Have a few volunteers share their thinking with the class.

Explain that each student will write his own nonfiction piece about the season he discussed with his partner. Explain that partners may talk to each other during the writing time about what they will write.

WRITING TIME

 Write About Spring, Summer, or Fall Where They Live

Have the students return to desks, with partners sitting together. Have them open to the next blank page in their writing notebooks. Have them talk quietly and write about their seasons for 20–30 minutes.

Join the students in writing for a few minutes. When the students are settled into their writing, confer with individual students.

TEACHER CONFERENCE NOTE

Continue to confer with individual students about their nonfiction writing. Ask each student to read her piece aloud to you as you ask yourself:

- Can I tell what the topic is?

- Is the student writing factual information about the topic?

- Is the writing clear? Does it make sense?

Support students by reading their writing back to them and asking them questions such as:

Q *Does the writing make sense? What do you need to change so it makes sense?*

Q *What more can you tell about [what you do on fall holidays]?*

Document your observations for each student using the "Conference Notes" record sheet (BLM1).

Signal to let the students know when writing time is over.

SHARING AND REFLECTING

4 ▶ Share Sentences and Reflect

Ask the students to quietly read their writing and each underline a sentence to share with the class. After allowing time for them to choose their sentences, go around the room and have each student read his underlined sentence aloud, without comment.

Ask and briefly discuss:

Q *What did you hear that got you interested in someone else's writing?*

Q *What questions do you want to ask [Reggie] about what [he] wrote?*

Explain that tomorrow the students will think about what more they can add to their writing about seasons.

EXTENSION

Learn More About Cindy Lou Aillaud

Cindy Lou Aillaud, a former kindergarten teacher, is now an elementary school physical education teacher in Alaska. Learn more about how she became an author by searching the Internet using the keywords "Cindy Lou Aillaud."

Day 3

Exploring Nonfiction and Conferring in Pairs

In this lesson, the students:

- Reread their writing and add descriptive language
- Express interest in and appreciation for one another's writing
- Tell what more they want to know about one another's writing
- Give feedback in a helpful way
- Thank one another for their help

Materials

- *Recess at 20 Below*

GETTING READY TO WRITE

1 ▶ Discuss Descriptive Language

Have partners get their writing notebooks and sit together at desks today. Show *Recess at 20 Below* and remind the students that they heard this book yesterday. Tell the students that you will reread a page, and ask them to close their eyes and listen for words that help them imagine what's happening. Read page 5 aloud twice ("The cold takes my breath away…"). Ask and briefly discuss:

Q *What did you see in your mind? What words helped you see this?*

Q *What sounds did you hear? What words helped you hear those sounds?*

Point out that the author includes a lot of descriptive words to help the reader imagine what winter is like in Alaska.

◀ **Teacher Note**

As the students respond, reread the corresponding passages aloud.

2 ▶ Reread Writing and Add Descriptive Language

Ask the students to quietly reread their pieces about spring, summer, or fall and to look up when they are finished. When most students have finished reading, use "Think, Pair, Share" to have partners first think about and then discuss:

Teacher Note ▶

Pause long enough after each question to allow the students to review their writing.

 Q *What descriptive words can you add to help your reader see what your season is like?* [pause] *Turn to your partner.*

 Q *What descriptive words can you add to help your reader hear your season?* [pause] *Turn to your partner.*

 Q *What descriptive words can you add to help your reader smell or taste your season?* [pause] *Turn to your partner.*

Without discussing the questions as a class, explain that the students will add descriptive words to their nonfiction pieces during writing time today.

WRITING TIME

3 ▶ Add Descriptive Language to Pieces About Seasons

Have the students work quietly on their pieces for 20–30 minutes. If they finish, they may choose another season and write about it. Join the students in writing for a few minutes. When the students are settled into their writing, confer with individual students.

TEACHER CONFERENCE NOTE

Continue to confer with individual students about their nonfiction writing. Ask each student to read his piece aloud to you as you ask yourself:

* Can I tell what the topic is?

* Is the student writing factual information about the topic?

* Is the writing clear? Does it make sense?

continues

> **TEACHER CONFERENCE NOTE** *continued*
>
> Support students by reading their writing back to them and asking them questions such as:
>
> **Q** *Does the writing make sense? What do you need to change so it makes sense?*
>
> **Q** *What more can you tell about [what you like to eat in the summer]?*
>
> Document your observations for each student using the "Conference Notes" record sheet (BLM1).

Signal to let the students know when writing time is over.

SHARING AND REFLECTING

 Confer in Pairs

Gather the class with partners sitting together, facing you. Explain that partners will read their pieces to each other and tell each other what they like about the other's piece and what else they want to know.

Give partners several minutes to share and discuss their pieces. When most pairs have finished sharing, signal for the students' attention. Ask and briefly discuss:

Q *What did your partner like about your piece?*

Q *What was one thing your partner wanted to know about your piece?*

Have the students take a moment to add any information they can about what their partner wanted to know.

5▶ Reflect on Pair Conferences

Ask and briefly discuss:

Q *What did your partner do during your conference that was helpful to you?*

Remind the students that the purpose of pair conferences is for partners to help each other improve their writing. Encourage partners to thank each other for their help.

Day 4

Selecting Drafts and Conferring in Pairs

In this lesson, the students:

- Review their nonfiction writing from the unit
- Select pieces to complete and publish
- Add to their selected drafts
- Tell what more they want to know about one another's writing
- Give feedback in a helpful way
- Ask one another questions about their writing

Materials

- *Assessment Resource Book*

GETTING READY TO WRITE

1 ▶ Review and Select Drafts to Publish

Have the students begin the lesson at their desks today. Review that during the past four weeks they have heard and written nonfiction. Explain that today they will review all of the nonfiction pieces they have written and each select one to work on and publish as a book for the classroom library.

Explain that the piece they select does not yet need to be finished. Encourage them to select a piece that interests them and that they think will be interesting for other students to read. Have the students open their notebooks, reread the nonfiction pieces they have written, and each select one to work on and publish.

As the students review their work, circulate and observe. Support individual students by asking them questions such as:

Q *Which is your favorite piece of nonfiction? What do you like about it?*

Q *What more might you add to this piece to finish it?*

After a few minutes, signal for the students' attention.

 Confer in Pairs

Explain that partners will read their pieces to each other and help each other by telling what more they want to know. Ask:

Q *Why will it be helpful to have your partner tell you what more he or she wants to know about your piece?*

Q *What is a helpful way you can tell your partner what more you want to know?*

Have partners read their pieces to each other and take turns telling each other what more they want to know. After several minutes, signal for the students' attention. Ask:

Q *What is one thing your partner wants to know that you might add to your piece?*

Have several volunteers share their thinking with the class. Explain that during writing time today, the students will add to their selected nonfiction pieces. Remind them to think about what more their partner wanted to know. If they finish, they may work on another piece of nonfiction writing.

WRITING TIME

Work on Nonfiction Pieces

Have the students work silently on their nonfiction pieces for 20–30 minutes. Join them in writing for a few minutes, and then walk around and observe.

CLASS ASSESSMENT NOTE

Observe the students as they work. Ask yourself:

- Are the students adding to their writing?

- Do they have a sense of when their pieces are finished?

If students are having difficulty, support them by having them tell you what they plan to add. Ask:

Q *Why did you pick this piece to publish? Why do you think your readers will find it interesting?*

Q *What did your partner suggest that you add? Where might you add that?*

Q *What else might you tell about your topic?*

Record your observations in the *Assessment Resource Book*.

Signal to let the students know when writing time is over.

SHARING AND REFLECTING

4 ▶ Share Sentences and Reflect

Explain that the students will each choose a sentence to share with the class. Ask the students to quietly read their writing and underline a sentence they think will interest their reader. After allowing a moment for them to choose, go around the room and have each student read her underlined sentence aloud, without comment.

Ask and briefly discuss:

Q *What did you hear that got you interested in someone else's writing?*

Q *What questions do you want to ask [Ronah] about what [she] wrote?*

Remind the students that next week they will make their pieces into books for the classroom library.

Teacher Note

If you have students that need more time to finish writing their nonfiction pieces, plan time for them to do this before beginning Week 5.

Week 5 Overview

UNIT 4: NONFICTION

Writing Focus

• Students proofread for spelling, punctuation, and capitalization.

• Students explore expository text features.

• Students write and illustrate final versions.

• Students publish their nonfiction writing as books.

• Students present their books from the Author's Chair.

Social Focus

• Students help one another improve their writing.

• Students act in fair and caring ways.

• Students work in a responsible way.

• Students listen respectfully to the thinking of others and share their own.

• Students express interest in and appreciation for one another's writing.

DO AHEAD

• Prior to Day 3, determine how the students will make their books, and gather the necessary materials in a central location. (See Unit 3, Week 4, Day 1, on page 284 for a simple procedure for making a final version into a book.) Decide on the procedure you would like the students to follow to access and return the materials.

TEACHER AS WRITER

"To me, writing a book is a great voyage of discovery; what attracts me to a subject in part is what I don't know about it, what I can learn from it."
— David McCullough

Think about the piece you wrote last week. What have you learned about the topic that surprised you? What are you curious about now? Jot your reflections in your notebook, and continue researching and writing more about this topic.

Day 1

Materials

- *Student Writing Handbooks*

Informal Proofreading and Conferring in Pairs

In this lesson, the students:

- Proofread their nonfiction pieces for spelling
- Proofread their nonfiction pieces for punctuation and capitalization
- Confer to make sure that their writing makes sense
- Give feedback in a helpful way

GETTING READY TO WRITE

1 ▶ Discuss Proofreading for Spelling

Have partners gather their writing notebooks and *Student Writing Handbooks* and sit together at desks today. Review that the students each selected a piece of nonfiction writing to publish for the classroom library. Remind them that published writing must be as free of errors as possible, and explain that they will check their spelling and punctuation today to make sure it is correct.

Ask the students to open to their nonfiction pieces and reread them, circling any words they are unsure how to spell. Stop the students after a couple of minutes and ask:

Q *What words have you circled so far?*

Have several volunteers report the words they circled. Ask the students to open their *Student Writing Handbooks* to the word bank, and remind them that this section contains an alphabetical list of correctly spelled, high-frequency words that students their age might use. Ask them to use the word bank to look up the first word they circled, and, if the word is there, to correct the spelling in their draft, if needed.

Teacher Note

If the students have difficulty looking up words in the word bank, take time to review dictionary skills with them. Write a word on the board and look up that word together as a class. Repeat with other words, if necessary.

Ask:

Q *If the word does not appear in the word bank, what else might you do to check the correct spelling?*

Students might say:

"I could ask someone at my table if they know how to spell it."

"I could ask my partner."

"I could ask you."

"If I know where I read that word in a book, I can go look it up there."

"I could look it up in a dictionary."

Remind the students that they will add any new words they learn how to spell to the word bank by writing them on the blank lines under the appropriate letter.

Explain that during writing time today the students will each check and correct the spelling in their piece. If they are sure that all their spelling is correct, they may set the piece aside and work on another piece of nonfiction.

WRITING TIME

2 Check Spelling

Have the students work on checking their spelling for 10–15 minutes. As they work, confer with individual students.

TEACHER CONFERENCE NOTE

Confer with individual students about the pieces they are developing for publication. Ask each student to read her piece aloud to you as you ask yourself:

- Can I tell what the topic is?

- Is the student writing factual information about the topic?

continues

TEACHER CONFERENCE NOTE *continued*

- Is the writing clear? Does it make sense?

- Does the student recognize misspelled words and correct them?

- Does the student capitalize the first letters of sentences and use periods at the ends?

Support students by reading their writing back to them and asking them questions such as:

Q *Does the writing make sense? What do you need to change so it makes sense?*

Q *What more can you tell about your topic?*

Be ready to show the students how to edit for punctuation, if necessary.

Document your observations for each student using the "Conference Notes" record sheet (BLM1).

▶3 Read Aloud and Check Punctuation

Signal for the students' attention and explain that you would like them to reread their pieces aloud (using soft voices) to make sure that they have used punctuation at the end of each sentence and capitalized the first letters of sentences. Also remind them to capitalize all names.

Have the students reread and check their punctuation; then give them several more minutes to finish proofreading their drafts for punctuation and spelling.

Signal to let the students know when writing time is over.

SHARING AND REFLECTING

4 ▶ Briefly Reflect as a Class

Ask and briefly discuss:

Q *What words did you check the spelling for today?*

Q *What words did you find in your word bank? How did you check on words that were not in the word bank?*

Q *What words did you capitalize? Why did you capitalize them?*

5 ▶ Confer in Pairs

Explain that partners will read their pieces to each other and help each other by making sure that everything makes sense. Write the question *Does it make sense?* where everyone can see it, and read the question aloud together. Explain that they should ask themselves this question as they listen to their partner read. Ask and briefly discuss:

Q *If something is confusing or doesn't make sense in your partner's piece, how can you tell him or her in a helpful way?*

> **Students might say:**
>
> "I could say, 'I didn't understand that part. Could you please read it again?'"
>
> "I could tell my partner why I'm confused."
>
> "I can help my partner figure out what to write so it makes sense."

Have partners read their pieces to each other and check to make sure everything makes sense. After several minutes, signal for the students' attention. Ask and briefly discuss:

Q *What is one thing your partner did to help you? Why was that helpful?*

Give the students a few moments to make any changes to their pieces based on what their partner said, and then have them put their writing away. Explain that tomorrow they will begin writing their final versions.

Day 2

Materials

- *How to Be a Friend* from Week 1
- *Polar Lands* from Week 3
- Loose, lined paper
- Drawing paper
- Crayons or colored markers

FACILITATION TIP

Reflect on your experience over the past few weeks with **asking facilitative questions**. Does this technique feel comfortable and natural to you? Do you find yourself using it throughout the school day? What effect has using this technique had on your students' listening and participation in discussions? We encourage you to continue to use and reflect on this technique throughout the year.

Writing Final Versions

In this lesson, the students:

- Explore illustrations and diagrams in nonfiction
- Determine where to add illustrations
- Write and illustrate final versions

GETTING READY TO WRITE

1 ▸ Explore Illustrations and Diagrams in Nonfiction

Have the students stay at their seats today. Explain that they will start writing the final versions of their nonfiction pieces. Remind them that these pieces will be made into books for the classroom library.

Remind the students that illustrations and diagrams are a common feature of many nonfiction books. Show the cover of *How to Be a Friend* and remind the students that in addition to the written text, the author uses illustrations to help the reader learn about being a friend. Read a few pages of the text and show the accompanying illustrations. Ask and briefly discuss:

Q *How do the illustrations help the reader?*

Show the cover of *Polar Lands* and explain that nonfiction authors sometimes use diagrams to present information. Turn to page 7 and read the text titled "Arctic" aloud. Show the diagram of the Arctic and read some of its labels aloud. Repeat this with the text titled "Antarctic" and the accompanying diagram. Ask:

Q *What information do these diagrams give the reader?*

Q *How is the information the same as the information in the text? How is it different?*

Students might say:

"The diagrams show some of the animals and where they live."

"I agree with [Stephanie]. In addition, they show the oceans and the poles."

"The diagrams are just like the text because they give information about what the Arctic and Antarctic are made of."

"I agree with [Craig], but they are different, too. The diagrams give information that is not in the text, like showing the animals that live there."

Turn to page 17 and read "Arctic Food Chain" aloud. Show the accompanying diagram and read its labels aloud. Ask:

Q *How is the information in this diagram the same as the information in the text? How is it different?*

Students might say:

"The diagram shows in pictures what the text says."

"Both the text and the pictures have the same information. One just uses words and the other uses pictures and words."

2 ▶ Reread Nonfiction Pieces and Discuss Adding Diagrams

Have the students reread their pieces and think about where they might draw illustrations or diagrams to help the reader. Use "Think, Pair, Share" to have partners first think about and then discuss:

 Q *Where might you include an illustration or diagram to give more information in your nonfiction book?* [pause] *Turn to your partner.*

After a moment, signal for the students' attention and have them write a star on their draft to remind them of something they want to illustrate in their final version.

Explain that the students will begin writing their final versions during writing time today. Show the lined paper and explain that they will copy their pieces in their best handwriting onto this paper. Show the drawing paper and explain that they will use it for their illustrations or diagrams.

WRITING TIME

3 ▶ Write and Illustrate Final Versions

Distribute the paper and have the students work for 20–30 minutes to write and illustrate their final versions. As they work, confer with individual students.

TEACHER CONFERENCE NOTE

Continue to confer with individual students about the pieces they are developing for publication. Ask each student to read his piece aloud to you as you ask yourself:

* Can I tell what the topic is?

* Is the student writing factual information about the topic?

* Is the writing clear? Does it make sense?

* Does the student recognize misspelled words and correct them?

* Does the student capitalize the first letters of sentences and use periods at the ends?

Support students by reading their writing back to them and asking them questions such as:

Q *Does the writing make sense? What do you need to change so it makes sense?*

Q *What more can you tell about your topic?*

Be ready to show the students how to edit for punctuation, if necessary.

Document your observations for each student using the "Conference Notes" record sheet (BLM1).

Signal to let the students know when writing time is over.

SHARING AND REFLECTING

 Reflect on Adding Illustrations or Diagrams

Have a few volunteers show and explain their illustrations or diagrams. Ask:

Q *How will your [illustration/diagram] help your reader?*

Explain that tomorrow the students will finish their final versions and make them into books. Have them place their final versions in their writing folders.

EXTENSION

Technology Tip: Publishing Student Writing Online

Some students might be interested in publishing their writing online for family members and friends to read. To search for websites where the students can do so, use the keywords "publishing children's writing."

Day 3

Materials

- Read-aloud books from this unit
- Loose, lined paper
- Drawing paper
- Crayons or colored markers
- Construction paper for book covers
- Stapler
- *Assessment Resource Book*

Publishing

In this lesson, the students:

- Explore features of nonfiction books
- Complete final versions of their nonfiction pieces
- Make their nonfiction pieces into books
- Handle materials responsibly
- Share materials fairly

GETTING READY TO WRITE

 Discuss Procedures for Making Books

Have the students stay at their seats today. Explain that they will finish writing and illustrating their final versions today, and then they will make these final versions into books. Explain the procedure you would like the students to follow to make their books, and how you would like them to access and return the bookmaking materials (see "Do Ahead" on page 387). Ask and briefly discuss:

Q *If someone is using something that you need, what might you do?*

Q *If you are using something that someone else needs, what might you do?*

 Discuss Book Covers and Features of Nonfiction Books

Point out that the students need to decide what they will include on their book covers. Ask and briefly discuss:

Q *What information is on the cover of a book? What else is on the cover?*

Explain that the students also need to decide whether they will add any of the features that professional authors sometimes include in their books. Use the read-aloud books from this unit to show and remind them of features such as the title page, dedication, author notes, table of contents, glossary, and back-cover blurbs. Tell the students that these books will be available during writing time so that they can look at these features more closely and include them in their own books if they wish.

WRITING TIME

3▶ Complete Final Versions and Make Books

Have the students work for 20–30 minutes to finish writing and illustrating the final versions of their pieces and begin making their books. Circulate, observe, and assist as needed.

CLASS ASSESSMENT NOTE

Observe the students and ask yourself:

- Are the students engaged and excited about making their nonfiction books?

- Do they include any features of nonfiction books?

- Do they handle the materials responsibly and share them fairly?

- If they have disputes about the materials, are they able to resolve them in a fair way?

Make note of any problems the students have so that you can discuss these problems at the end of the writing period. Also note whether most of the students will finish making their books today or whether they will need more time to do so.

Record your observations in the *Assessment Resource Book*.

Signal to let the students know when writing time is over.

SHARING AND REFLECTING

4 ▶ Reflect on Sharing Materials

Ask and briefly discuss:

Q *What did you notice about how we shared our bookmaking materials today?*

Q *What problems did we have? What do we want to do [the same way/differently] the next time we share materials?*

Share any observations you had with the class.

Explain that tomorrow the students will share their books from the Author's Chair. Have them put their books in their writing folders.

Teacher Note

If most of the students have completed their books, then conduct the Author's Chair sharing activity tomorrow, as suggested. If not, provide another day for the students to complete their books before proceeding with the Day 4 lesson.

Day 4

Publishing

In this lesson, the students:

- Present their books from the Author's Chair
- Give their full attention to the person who is speaking
- Ask one another questions about their writing
- Thank one another for their help
- Write freely

Materials

- Author's Chair

GETTING READY TO SHARE

1 Review Nonfiction

Gather the class with partners sitting together, facing the Author's Chair. Have them bring completed books with them. Explain that during the past five weeks, the students learned about nonfiction and wrote many nonfiction pieces. First in pairs, and then as a class, discuss:

 Q *What have you learned about nonfiction writing? Turn to your partner.*

 Q *What have you enjoyed about writing nonfiction? Turn to your partner.*

Remind the students that writers become better over time as they practice writing again and again. Encourage the students to continue to write about nonfiction topics they are interested in on their own and during their free writing time.

2▶ Review Responsible Behavior During Author's Chair Sharing

Review how the students will act during Author's Chair sharing, both as presenting authors and as members of the audience. Ask and discuss:

Q *What is important to do when presenting your book? Why is that important?*

Q *What is important to do as a member of the audience? Why is that important?*

SHARING TIME

3▶ Share Books from the Author's Chair

Ask for a volunteer who has completed his book to read it aloud from the Author's Chair. Facilitate a discussion using questions such as those below, and give the author an opportunity to respond to classmates' questions and comments.

Q *What is something you learned about [being a friend] from [Angelo's] book?*

Q *What did you imagine as you listened?*

Q *How did the illustrations help you understand the book?*

Q *What questions can we ask [Angelo] about [his] book?*

Follow this procedure to have other students share from the Author's Chair.

REFLECTING

 Reflect on Responsible Behavior

Ask:

Q *What did you do to be responsible when sharing from the Author's Chair? How did that help the audience?*

Q *What did you do to be a responsible audience member? How did that help the author? How did that help the other audience members?*

 Thank Each Other for Their Help

Ask:

 Q *What did you enjoy about working with your partner during this unit? Turn and tell your partner.*

Ask partners to thank each other for their help and good work together during the unit.

FREE WRITING TIME

 Write Freely

Explain that the students will have time now to write freely about anything they choose. Tell them that they may continue a piece they started earlier or begin a new piece. If they need help thinking of an idea to write about, they can look at the writing ideas section of their notebook.

Teacher Note

Repeat today's lesson for a few more days, or even another week, to give all of the students time to finish publishing their pieces and presenting them from the Author's Chair (see "Open Weeks" in the front matter of volume 1, page xvi).

Teacher Note

This is the end of Unit 4. Assign new partners before starting Unit 5.

Unit 5

Letter Writing

Unit 5

Letter Writing

During this three-week unit, the students read, discuss, and write friendly letters, including letters to one another, the teacher, first graders, family members, and friends. As they write, they consider the audience and purpose of their letters, as well as their choice of words. Throughout the unit, the students work responsibly, listen to the ideas of others, and share their own thinking.

UNIT OVERVIEW

WEEK	DAY 1	DAY 2	DAY 3	DAY 4
1	**Exploring Letter Writing:** *First Year Letters* **Focus:** • Writing letters to the teacher in pairs	**Exploring Letter Writing:** *First Year Letters* **Focus:** • Writing friendly letters to partners	**Exploring Letter Writing** **Focus:** • Setting up a classroom post office • Writing replies to partners' letters	**Exploring Letter Writing:** *First Year Letters* **Focus:** • Identifying parts of a friendly letter • Writing a shared letter to first graders
2	**Exploring Letter Writing** **Focus:** • Punctuating dates, greetings, and closings • Writing letters to classmates	**Exploring Letter Writing:** *Dear Baby* **Focus:** • Exploring audience and purpose • Writing to family members	**Exploring Letter Writing** **Focus:** • Listening for periods • Proofreading cards or letters for punctuation	**Drafting Friendly Letters:** *Love, Lizzie* **Focus:** • Choosing recipients for friendly letters • Drafting letters
3	**Informal Proofreading:** *First Year Letters* **Focus:** • Practicing proofreading • Completing draft letters • Proofreading draft letters	**Writing Final Versions** **Focus:** • Writing final versions of letters	**Publishing** **Focus:** • Addressing envelopes • Sharing from the Author's Chair	**Publishing** **Focus:** • Reflecting on writing letters • Sharing from the Author's Chair • Writing freely

UNIT 5: LETTER WRITING

First Year Letters
by Julie Danneberg, illustrated by Judy Love
(Charlesbridge, 2003)

Mrs. Sarah Jane Hartwell sets up a classroom post office to help her students practice writing letters.

Writing Focus

• Students hear, read, and discuss friendly letters.

• Students explore the parts of a friendly letter.

• Students explore audience and purpose.

• Students write letters to their partners, the teacher, and first graders.

Social Focus

• Students work in a responsible way.

• Students listen respectfully to the thinking of others and share their own.

• Students make decisions and solve problems respectfully.

DO AHEAD

• Prior to Day 1, decide how you will randomly assign partners to work together during the unit. See the front matter in volume 1 for suggestions about assigning partners randomly (page xiii) and for considerations for pairing English Language Learners (page xxvii).

• Prior to Day 1, write a letter to the class introducing the unit (see the diagram on page 409), seal it in an envelope, and address it to the class.

• Prior to Day 3, determine how and where to set up a classroom post office. It may be a single box on your desk or envelopes taped to a wall, one for each student and one for you. On Day 3, the class will decide the procedures for using the post office, such as when and how to "mail" letters, and when and how to check for or distribute them. Think ahead about these issues. (If you already have a classroom post office, use it and the procedures you've established for it.)

• Make sure you have loose, lined writing paper available for the students to use to write letters throughout the unit.

TEACHER AS WRITER

"…I write not so much because I have anything to say, as because I hope for an answer; and the vacancy of my life makes a letter of great value."
— Samuel Johnson

How often do you receive a friendly letter? Think about a time when you waited eagerly for a letter to arrive or were surprised or excited to receive a letter. Write about what happened and what that letter meant to you.

Day 1

Materials

- *First Year Letters*
- Letter to the class in a sealed envelope (see "Do Ahead" on page 407)
- Loose, lined paper
- *Assessment Resource Book*

Exploring Letter Writing

In this lesson, the students:

- Work with a new partner
- Hear and discuss friendly letters
- Informally explore audience and purpose
- Write friendly letters to the teacher in pairs
- Work responsibly in pairs

About Teaching Letter Writing

In this unit, the students are introduced to friendly letters. They learn the standard format for a friendly letter (date, greeting, body, closing, and signature), consider the audience and purpose when writing, and write letters and cards. As they write, they think about how their use of words will affect the receiver, and they work to capture the tone of friendly conversation in their letters.

During the first two weeks of this unit, the students hear and write many letters. They learn how to punctuate friendly letters and practice doing so. At the end of the second week, they begin drafting letters that they will revise and publish (and possibly mail) during the third week.

GETTING READY TO WRITE

1▶ Introduce Letter Writing

Teacher Note

The partners you assign today will stay together for the unit.

Making Meaning® Teacher

You can either have the students work with their current *Making Meaning* partner or assign them a different partner for the writing lessons.

Randomly assign partners (see "Do Ahead" on page 407). Gather the class with partners sitting together, facing you.

Hold up the sealed envelope and state that the class has received a letter. Open the envelope and read the letter aloud.

                                    February 15

Dear class,

    Today we are starting a new writing unit. We will learn about writing letters. We will write many letters, some to each other and some to our family and friends. We will receive letters, too.

    I can't wait to get a letter from each of you!

                                    Your teacher,

                                    Mrs. Peterson

Ask and briefly discuss:

Q *Who is this letter written to? Who is it from?*

Q *What did you learn from this letter?*

2 ▶ Read and Discuss *First Year Letters*

Explain that you will read a book about students who write letters to their teacher. Show the cover of *First Year Letters* and read the title and the names of the author and the illustrator aloud. Read the blurb on the back cover of the book, and then explain that this book is titled *First Year Letters* because this is Mrs. Hartwell's first year as a teacher.

Read the book aloud, showing the illustrations and stopping as indicated. Clarify vocabulary as you read.

> **Suggested Vocabulary**
>
> **detention:** punishment in which students must stay inside at recess or after school (p. 11)
>
> **smithereens:** very small pieces (p. 14)
>
> **aquarium:** building with displays of fish and other water animals (p. 21)
>
> **refrain:** stop yourself, hold back (p. 24)

◀ **Teacher Note**

The illustrations in *First Year Letters* are important to understanding the story. Take time to show and discuss what is happening in them. When reading page 18, it might help to explain that the class is celebrating Groundhog Day.

Stop after:

> **p. 3**   "Thanks, Shannon"

Ask and briefly discuss:

Q   *Why might the teacher, Mrs. Hartwell, be a little scared?*

Reread page 3 and continue reading. Stop after:

> **p. 6**   "Sincerely, Carl"

Ask and briefly discuss:

Q   *Who do you think Mrs. Burton is, and what is she doing?*

Reread page 6 and continue reading. Stop after:

> **p. 13**   "P.S. When you wear your safety goggles, you look just like my frog, Benny."

Ask and briefly discuss:

Q   *What happened during science class?*

Reread page 13 and continue reading to the end of the book. Ask and briefly discuss:

Q   *How is this book written differently from most of the books we have read?*

▶ 3 Think Before Writing

Show page 5 and remind the students that Andy tells Mrs. Hartwell some things he thinks are important for teachers to know. Reread the page and ask:

 Q   *If you were going to write me a letter about important things I should know to make our class better, what might you write? Turn to your partner.*

Teacher Note ▶

If necessary, explain that Mrs. Burton is the principal and she is observing Mrs. Hartwell teach.

 ELL **Note**

If necessary, simplify this question by rephrasing it in the following way:

Q   *Andy told his teacher what he would like her to do to make their class better. What would you like me to do to make our class better?*

Signal for the students' attention and have several volunteers share with the class.

> **Students might say:**
>
> "My partner and I said we need enough playground balls so everyone who wants a ball can play with one."
>
> "We need a snack in the morning. We would write that."
>
> "We would write: *Please pick us up from the playground right after the bell rings because we get cold.*"
>
> "We'd like more computer time."

Explain that today you would like each pair to write you a letter telling you some things they think would make the class better. (Partners will work together to write one letter from both of them to you.)

Mention that during writing time today you will observe how partners work together and then will talk with the students about what you notice. Ask and briefly discuss:

Q *How will you and your partner work responsibly?*

> **Students might say:**
>
> "We'll get to work right away."
>
> "I agree with [Sophia], and we'll work quiety and not bother our neighbors."
>
> "In addition to what [Edgar] said, we'll listen to each other and agree on what we write."
>
> "I agree with everyone so far, and another way to work responsibly is to share the work."

Encourage the students to keep these things in mind as they work today.

WRITING TIME

4▶ Write Letters in Pairs

Distribute lined writing paper and have partners move to sit together at desks and work on their letters to you. Explain that partners will talk

---

◀ Teacher Note

If the students have difficulty generating ideas, stimulate their thinking by suggesting some of the ideas in the "Students might say" note.

◀ Teacher Note

The standard features of a friendly letter (date, greeting, and so on) will be introduced on Day 4 of this week. The focus for the first three days is for the students to write freely without undue concern for the format of letters. Observe to see what features, if any, the students do use.

Teacher Note

If necessary, remind the students to use the discussion prompts they have learned:

- "I agree with _____ because…"
- "I disagree with _____ because…"
- "In addition to what _____ said, I think…"

Teacher Note

You might explain that during this unit the students will write letters that they will give or send to others, so they will write on loose paper rather than in their writing notebooks.

softly to each other during writing time today. As pairs work, circulate and observe.

CLASS ASSESSMENT NOTE

Observe partners and ask yourself:

* Do partners start writing quickly and stay on task?

* Do they share the work?

* Do they agree on what to write?

Support pairs who are struggling to write by asking questions such as:

Q *What is something you'd like me to know about [our classroom/our classroom rules/how we go to lunch/how we use the computers]?*

Q *What should I know about recess time? What are some things that could make recess time better?*

As you observe, jot a few notes about ways the students work responsibly and any problems you notice. You will use these notes during the reflection time at the end of the lesson.

Record your observations in the *Assessment Resource Book*.

After 15–20 minutes, signal for the students' attention. Ask partners to read their letters aloud softly; then ask:

 Q *Does your letter make sense? If not, what changes do you need to make? Turn to your partner.*

 Q *What else do you want to tell me about how to make our class better? Turn to your partner.*

Give partners another 10–15 minutes to make any changes and finish their letters.

Signal to let the students know when writing time is over.

SHARING AND REFLECTING

5 ▶ **Reflect on Partner Work**

Explain that you would like each pair to share with the class one thing they wanted you to know. Give partners a moment to decide which partner will share and what to share, and then go around the room and have the designated partner in each pair read the selected item aloud. Ask and briefly discuss:

Q   *What did you hear that you agree with? Why do you agree?*

Q   *How did your partner work go today? What went well? What do you need to work on?*

Share some of the things that you noticed when observing the students work.

Collect the letters and tell the students that you will read them. Explain that the class will continue to explore letter writing tomorrow.

◀ **Teacher Note**

Read the students' letters before teaching the Day 2 lesson and think about the letter you will write in response (see the example on page 415). Also notice which features of a letter most of the students already use and which they do not use.

EXTENSION

Respond to Literature

Show and reread the sign on page 17 in *First Year Letters* aloud: "In this classroom everyone is a student, everyone is a teacher." First in pairs, and then as a class, discuss the meaning of these words. If necessary, offer examples of how everyone in the class is both a student and a teacher. Then invite the students to write about what these words mean to them. Alternately, you might reread the letter on page 17 and invite the students to write about what Alexandra's mother means when she tells Alexandra "to do a little less teaching and a little more learning."

Day 2

Materials

- *First Year Letters*
- Chart paper and a marker

Exploring Letter Writing

In this lesson, the students:

- Hear, read, and discuss friendly letters
- Write friendly letters to their partners
- Use writing time responsibly

GETTING READY TO WRITE

 Model Writing a Letter

Gather the class with partners sitting together, facing you. Show *First Year Letters* and remind the students that they heard this book and then wrote letters to you about what they think you should know that would make the class better. Explain that you have read their letters and that you will now write a letter back to the class.

On a sheet of lined chart paper, write a letter that responds to some of the things the students wrote to you in their letters (see the diagram). As you write, read your letter aloud and discuss:

Q *What do you notice about my writing that tells you that this is a letter?*

Students might say:

"After the date, you start with 'Dear class.'"

"I agree with [Scarlett]. When you see 'Dear Somebody,' you know it's a letter."

"After that, you tell something or ask a question."

"In addition to what [Randy] said, at the end of the letter, you sign your name."

February 16

Dear class,

    I enjoyed reading your letters. Something I learned is that our rabbit cage is smelly and needs to be cleaned more often. I also learned that many of you would like more computer time. What ideas do you have about how to do these things?

    Please write to me again!

Yours truly,

Mrs. Peterson

Explain that this is a *friendly letter*, a type of letter people write to friends, family members, and other people they like. Reread the letter aloud; then ask:

Q *How does reading this letter make you feel? What in the letter makes you feel that way?*

Students might say:

"It made me feel good that you liked reading our letters."

"You use nice words like 'please' and 'thank you.' That feels friendly."

"I agree with [Cynthia]. The letter sounds friendly, like you are talking to us."

"In addition to what [Diego] said, you ask us a question."

"It made me want to write back."

Explain that friendly letters are like pleasant conversations in writing. Tell the students that today partners will write each other friendly letters. Tomorrow they will read and reply to the letters.

2▶ Generate Ideas for Partner Letters

Explain that friendly letters help people get to know one another, so in their friendly letters partners should tell something about themselves. Ask and briefly discuss:

Q *What is something you can tell your partner about yourself in your letter?*

Q *What is something you can ask your partner in your letter?*

Teacher Note ▶

If necessary, probe for ideas so that the "I can write about" and "I can ask" lists are not identical.

As the students respond, record their ideas on a sheet of chart paper under the headings *I can write about* and *I can ask*.

I can write about:

My family

My favorite things

Things I like to do after school or on the weekend

What I want to do during summer vacation

I can ask:

What do you like to play at recess?

What do you like to do with your family?

When is your bedtime? How do you get ready for bed?

Invite the students to look at this chart and the letter you wrote to the class to help them get ideas for their letters today.

WRITING TIME

 Write Friendly Letters

Distribute lined writing paper and have the students return to their seats. Have them work silently on letters to their partners for 20–30 minutes.

Join the students in writing for a few minutes, and then circulate and observe.

Signal to let the students know when writing time is over.

SHARING AND REFLECTING

 Reflect on Writing Letters

Ask:

 Q *How is writing a letter to your partner the same as or different from talking to him or her? Turn to your partner.*

After a few moments, signal for the students' attention and have a few volunteers share their thinking with the class.

> **Students might say:**
>
> "You can tell your partner about something when you talk or when you write a letter."
>
> "I agree with [Janice], and you can also ask a question when you talk or when you write a letter."
>
> "It's different because when I write a letter to my partner I have to wait until she writes me back. When I talk to her I don't have to wait."

Explain that tomorrow the students will mail their letters to their partners using a classroom post office. For now, have them place their letters in their writing folders and put their folders away until tomorrow.

◀ **Teacher Note**

If you notice students having difficulty writing, support them by asking them questions such as:

Q *What is something you want your partner to know about you? How can you write that as a sentence?*

Q *What is something you want to find out about your partner? How can you write that as a question?*

 Note

If you have two beginning English Language Learners in a pair who speak the same native language, consider having them write to each other in that language.

Teacher Note

Save your charted letter and the "I can write about/I can ask" chart to use throughout this unit.

Day 3

Materials

- *First Year Letters*
- Classroom post office (see "Do Ahead" on page 407)
- Your charted letter to the class from Day 2
- "I can write about/I can ask" chart from Day 2

Exploring Letter Writing

In this lesson, the students:

- Determine procedures for the classroom post office
- Read and discuss friendly letters
- Write friendly letters to their partners
- Make fair decisions
- Share what they learn about their partner

GETTING READY TO WRITE

▶1 Introduce the Classroom Post Office

Gather the class with partners sitting together, facing you. Show the cover of *First Year Letters* and review that the students in Mrs. Hartwell's class had a classroom post office. Direct their attention to the post office you have set up in the classroom (see "Do Ahead" on page 407) and explain that the students will have a chance to write letters to each other and mail them using this classroom post office.

Explain that the class needs to make some decisions about how to use the post office. Ask and discuss:

Q *When and how will we mail our letters? What can we do so everyone isn't mailing letters at the same time?*

Q *When and how will we deliver our letters?*

Q *What else do we need to do so everyone gets to use our classroom post office in a fair way?*

Have the students return to their seats and take out the letters they wrote yesterday. Follow the procedures established by the class to mail and deliver the letters.

Teacher Note

Depending on the type of post office you use, the students may need to fold their letters and put the recipient's name on the outside of each letter. You may need to show them how to do this. ▶

Ask and briefly discuss:

Q *How did our procedures for mailing and delivering letters work? What do we need to change?*

2 Prepare to Respond to Partner Letters

Explain that today the students will each read their partner's letter and write back, answering any questions. Remind the students to think as they write back about how their partner will feel when reading the letter. Ask and briefly discuss:

Q *What are some words you might use that will help your partner feel good when reading your friendly letter?*

Q *What can you do if you need help reading your partner's letter?*

Encourage the students to keep these things in mind as they work today. Direct their attention to your charted letter and the "I can write about/I can ask" chart from yesterday and encourage them to use these to help them write today.

WRITING TIME

3 Write Friendly Letters

Distribute lined writing paper and have the students read and write friendly letters for 20–30 minutes. If they finish writing to their partner, they may write a letter to the teacher or anyone else they choose.

Join the students in writing for a few minutes, and then circulate and observe.

Signal to let the students know when writing time is over.

FACILITATION TIP

During this unit, we invite you to focus on **pacing class discussions** so they are lively and focused without dragging, losing participants, or wandering off the topic. Class discussions should be long enough to allow time for thinking and short enough to sustain attention. Good pacing requires careful observation of the class (not just the students who are responding) and the timely use of various pacing techniques.

To speed up a discussion:

* Call on just a few students to respond to each question, even if others have their hands up.

* Use "Turn to Your Partner" if many students want to speak; then call on just two or three students to share with the whole class.

To deepen or refocus a discussion:

* Restate the original question if the discussion goes off the topic.

* Ask pairs to discuss whether they agree or disagree with what a classmate has just said.

* Use wait-time before calling on anyone to respond.

◀ **Teacher Note**

During writing time each day, you might write letters to one or two students and mail them in the classroom post office so each student receives a letter from you during this unit.

SHARING AND REFLECTING

 Reflect on Writing Letters and Working Responsibly

Ask and briefly discuss:

Q *What did you learn about your partner from his or her letter?*

Q *What friendly words did your partner use in his or her letter?*

Explain that the students will continue to explore letter writing tomorrow.

EXTENSION

Create a Letter Collection or a Letter-Writing Center

You might assemble a collection of letters for the students to browse. Bring in cards, notes, and letters from home, and consider asking the students to bring in any that they have received.

You might also create a letter-writing center with stationery and envelopes for the students to use to write letters to others in the class or to family and friends.

Day 4

Exploring Letter Writing

In this lesson, the students:

- Explore the parts of a friendly letter
- Write a shared letter to first graders
- Write letters to anyone else they choose
- Share their partner's writing with the class

GETTING READY TO WRITE

1 ▶ Explore the Parts of a Friendly Letter

Gather the class with partners sitting together, facing you. Direct their attention to your charted letter to the class and review that this is an example of a friendly letter. State that cards and thank you notes are also types of friendly letters.

Explain that a friendly letter has five parts. Point to each part on your charted letter (date, greeting, body, closing, and signature) and write the name of the part next to it. Point out that the students may already be using some of these parts, while some may be new to them.

Show and reread page 3 in *First Year Letters*, and then ask:

Q *What is the greeting in this letter?*

Q *What makes this a friendly letter?*

Q *How does this writer close the letter?*

Explain that there are many closings a writer of a friendly letter can use. Show and read the closings on pages 5, 6, 10, and 30 of *First Year Letters* and list these on the chart next to the word *closing*.

Materials

- *First Year Letters*
- Your charted letter to the class from Day 2
- Classroom post office from Day 3
- Chart paper and a marker
- *Assessment Resource Book*

◀ **Teacher Note**

The friendly letter format used in this unit includes the date, greeting, body, closing, and signature. If the format you teach differs from this format, use your format instead. Keep in mind that the goal is not for the students to be able to name the specific parts of a friendly letter, but for them to use a standard format when writing friendly letters.

Write a Shared Letter to a First Grade Class

Direct the students' attention to the date of the letter on page 3 of *First Year Letters* and remind them that Shannon wrote this letter on the first day of school. Ask and briefly discuss:

Q *How was Shannon feeling when she wrote this letter?*

Q *How have you felt on the first day of school?*

Point out that this year's first graders will likely feel a bit scared and nervous on the first day of second grade next year. Suggest that to help the first graders feel less scared, the class will write a friendly letter that welcomes them to second grade.

Write today's date on a sheet of chart paper and discuss:

Q *What shall we write as a greeting?*

Use the students' suggestions to write the greeting. Continue to use their suggestions to write the rest of the letter, discussing questions such as:

Q *How shall we start the body of our letter?*

Q *What can we tell the first graders that will help them look forward to second grade? How can we write that as a sentence?*

Q *What shall we write as our closing?*

Q *How shall we sign the letter?*

_____ February 18 __

Dear First graders in room 110, _____

     Next year, you will be in second grade. We want to tell

you about it. In second grade, you will be with some of the

same friends you have this year and probably meet some

new friends, too. You will take fun field trips and get better

at reading and math. You will learn new things like cursive

writing and multiplication. We love second grade and know

you will, too. _____

_____ Yours truly, _____

_____ The second graders __

_____ in room 202 ____

As a class, decide how to deliver the letter to the first grade class.

▶3 Prepare to Write Friendly Letters

Explain that today the students may write friendly letters to anyone they choose. Give the students a moment to decide who they will write their letters to. Then use "Think, Pair, Share" to have partners first think about and then discuss:

 Q *What do you want to tell this person in your letter?* [pause] *Turn to your partner.*

 Q *What do you want to ask this person in your letter?* [pause] *Turn to your partner.*

For each question, have a few volunteers share their thinking with the class. Reread your charted letter, pointing out the five parts (date, greeting, body, closing, signature); then remind the students to include these parts in their own letters. Tell them that they will share their letters in pairs after writing time. They may use your charted letter to the class or the letter to the first graders as a model.

WRITING TIME

4 ▸ Write Friendly Letters

Distribute lined writing paper and have the students return to their seats and work silently on their friendly letters for 20–30 minutes.

Join the students in writing for a few minutes; then circulate and observe.

CLASS ASSESSMENT NOTE

Observe the students and ask yourself:

* Do the students begin writing eagerly?

* Do they use the five parts of a friendly letter?

* Do they seem to consider the feelings of the recipient as they write?

Support students who are struggling by asking them questions such as:

Q *Look around the room. Who is someone you might write to?*

Q *What is something you might tell about yourself in this letter? How might you write that?*

Q *What is something you want to ask this person? What question can you write to ask that?*

Record your observations in the *Assessment Resource Book*.

Signal to let the students know when writing time is over.

SHARING AND REFLECTING

5 ▸ Reflect on Independent Writing

Have the students bring their letters and gather with partners sitting together, facing you. Explain that partners will read their letters to each other. Alert the students to listen carefully, as they will share something their partner wrote with the class.

Have partners tell each other who they wrote to and why, and then have them read their letters to each other.

Signal for the students' attention; then ask and briefly discuss:

Q *Who did your partner write to? What was something your partner told or asked that person in the letter?*

Explain that next week the students will continue to explore letter writing and will hear another book in which a story is told through friendly letters.

EXTENSION

Write to Pen Pals

Consider working with a first grade teacher to assign a first grader as a pen pal to each student in your class. Have the students write friendly letters to their pen pals, introducing themselves and telling something about their experience in second grade. You might also develop a pen pal relationship with another second grade class in another part of the country (or even another part of the world). Websites such as www.sincerelyyourspenpals.com, www.epals.com, and www.kidscom.com can help you connect with an interested class.

Teacher Note

Display your charted letter with the five parts of a letter identified for students to refer to throughout the unit.

Week 2 Overview

UNIT 5: LETTER WRITING

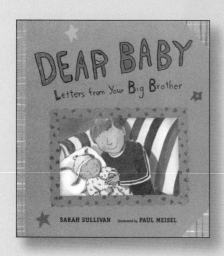

Dear Baby: Letters from Your Big Brother
by Sarah Sullivan, illustrated by Paul Meisel
(Candlewick Press, 2005)

Mike writes letters to his new sister before and after she is born.

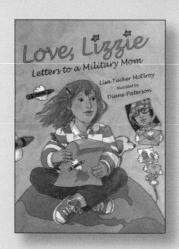

Love, Lizzie: Letters to a Military Mom
by Lisa Tucker McElroy, illustrated by Diane Paterson
(Albert Whitman & Company, 2005)

Lizzie's mom is stationed overseas, but Lizzie and her mom keep in touch with each other by writing letters.

Writing Focus

- Students hear, read, and discuss friendly letters.

- Students explore the parts of a friendly letter.

- Students explore punctuation in a friendly letter.

- Students explore audience and purpose.

- Students write cards and letters to classmates, family members, and acquaintances.

Social Focus

- Students reflect on their relationships to others.

- Students listen respectfully to the thinking of others and share their own.

- Students make decisions and solve problems respectfully.

DO AHEAD

- Prior to Day 1, write a letter to the class on a sheet of chart paper that reviews last week's work and previews this week's work (see the diagram on page 429).

- Prior to Day 1, write each student's name on a slip of paper, fold the slips of paper, and place them in a paper bag.

- Prior to Day 3, make transparencies of "Unpunctuated Letter 1" and "Unpunctuated Letter 2" (BLM4–BLM5).

- Prior to Day 4, consider previewing *Love, Lizzie* with your English Language Learners. Read it aloud and show and discuss the illustrations.

TEACHER AS WRITER

"…everybody who is human has something to express. Try not expressing yourself for twenty-four hours and see what happens. You will nearly burst. You will want to write a long letter or draw a picture or sing, or make a dress or a garden."

— Brenda Ueland

What are some of the ways you write friendly letters? Do you write them in the form of letters, cards, postcards, or e-mails? Think about someone you haven't contacted in a while and write that person a friendly letter. Think and write about what you would like him or her to know about your life, and ask questions about what you would like to know about his or her life.

Day 1

Materials

- Your charted letter to the class (see "Do Ahead" on page 427)

- Classroom post office from Week 1

- Bag with students' names on slips of paper (see "Do Ahead" on page 427)

Teacher Note ▶

If the students identify a problem with the post office procedures, take the time to discuss how to solve it.

Exploring Letter Writing

In this lesson, the students:

- Hear, read, and discuss a friendly letter

- Explore the parts of a friendly letter

- Explore how to punctuate a friendly letter

- Write friendly letters to classmates

- Discuss and solve problems that arise in their work together

- Imagine and discuss how others might feel

GETTING READY TO WRITE

 Discuss the Classroom Post Office

Gather the class with partners sitting together, facing you. Remind the students that last week they began using a classroom post office to mail letters to one another. Ask and briefly discuss:

Q *How is our post office working? What changes, if any, do we need to make?*

Q *Why is it important to write back to someone who writes to you?*

Q *In addition to independent writing time, when else can you write letters?*

Students might say:

"Our classroom post office is working really well. I like getting letters."

"I disagree with [Samantha]. I think that it is not working well, because some people are not getting letters."

"It is polite to write back to someone."

"In addition to what [Meiling] said, if you don't write back the person will wonder whether you got the letter."

"We can write during free writing time or when we finish our other work."

Ask the students to keep the things they discussed in mind as they write letters and use the classroom post office this week.

2 Discuss Punctuating Letters

Explain that you have written another letter to the class. Direct the students' attention to your charted letter and read it aloud.

February 22

Dear class,

    Last week, we began a unit about letter writing. We learned about the parts of a friendly letter. Do you remember what they are?

    This week, we will learn about punctuation in a friendly letter.

Sincerely yours,

Mrs. Peterson

Explain that letters require specific punctuation. Discuss:

Q *What do you notice about the punctuation marks in the date?*

Q *What do you notice about how the greeting is punctuated?*

Q *What punctuation is used in the closing?*

Explain that today the students will continue to write letters to one another. They will each draw a classmate's name from a bag and write that person a friendly letter. Encourage them to tell about themselves and to ask questions in their letters. Remind them to use the five parts of a friendly letter and to look at your charted letter for help with punctuation.

Call on the students to come up one at a time, draw a name from the bag, and return to their seats to begin writing.

FACILITATION TIP

Continue to focus on **pacing class discussions** so they are neither too short nor too long. Scan the whole class (not just the students who are responding) to assess participation and use techniques such as the following:

- Call on just a few students to respond to each question, even if others have their hands up.

- Use "Turn to Your Partner" if many students want to speak; then call on just two or three students to share with the whole class.

- Restate the original question if the discussion goes off the topic.

- Ask pairs to discuss whether they agree or disagree with what a classmate has just said.

- Use wait-time before calling on anyone to respond.

WRITING TIME

3 ▶ Write Independently

Have the students work silently on their letters for 15–20 minutes. Join the students in writing for a few minutes, and then begin conferring with individual students.

TEACHER CONFERENCE NOTE

During the next two weeks, confer with individual students by having each student read and tell you about his letter. Ask yourself:

* Does the student include all of the parts of a friendly letter?

* Does he tell about himself and ask questions?

* Does he correctly punctuate each part of the letter?

Support students by asking them questions such as:

Q *Who are you writing to? How will you greet [him/her]?*

Q *What can you say about yourself in your letter? What questions can you ask?*

Q *What punctuation will you use here?*

Q *How will you close your letter?*

Document your observations for each student using the "Conference Notes" record sheet (BLM1).

Signal for the students' attention. Ask the students to reread their letters and check their punctuation; then have them continue writing silently for a few more minutes. Students who finish writing their letters may write another letter to anyone they choose.

Signal to let the students know when writing time is over.

SHARING AND REFLECTING

 Reflect on Writing and One Another's Feelings

Ask and briefly discuss:

Q *What punctuation did you use today? Read us a place where you used [a comma]. Why did you need [a comma] here?*

Q *What friendly words did you include in your letter? How do you think your classmate will feel reading those words?*

Explain that tomorrow the students will hear another book with a story that is told through friendly letters. Have the students mail the letters they wrote using the classroom post office.

Teacher Note

Save your charted letter with punctuation to use throughout the unit.

Day 2

Materials

- *Dear Baby*
- Chart paper and a marker
- Your charted letter from Day 1

Exploring Letter Writing

In this lesson, the students:

- Hear and discuss friendly letters
- Explore audience and purpose
- Write letters or cards to family members
- Share their partner's writing with the class
- Give their full attention to the person who is speaking

GETTING READY TO WRITE

1 ▶ Read and Discuss *Dear Baby*

Gather the class with partners sitting together, facing you. Show *Dear Baby* and explain that this is another story told through friendly letters. Read the title (including the subtitle) and the names of the author and the illustrator aloud. Briefly discuss:

Q *What does this title tell you about this story?*

Show and read pages 2–7 aloud; then, referring to the letter on page 6, ask:

Q *In this letter, the greeting Mike writes is "Dear Erica." How is this different from the greeting in the earlier letters he wrote? Why did he change his greeting?*

Continue reading pages 8–23 aloud, showing the illustrations and clarifying vocabulary as you read.

Teacher Note ▶

You may wish to stop at various places throughout this book to discuss Mike's pictures and handwritten comments, and to discuss how Mike's feelings about the baby are changing.

Suggested Vocabulary

invisible: not able to be seen (p. 10)

disgusting: unattractive and unpleasant (p. 14)

After reading page 23, point out the "P.S." Explain that sometimes after someone has written a letter he thinks of something else he wants to say so he adds a *postscript*, which means "after writing." "P.S." is the abbreviation for *postscript*.

Show and read the letter on page 24; then ask and briefly discuss:

Q *What does Mike do in this letter that shows that this is* not *a friendly letter?*

Students might say:

"He uses capital letters for words he wants to shout."

"In addition to what [Eduardo] said, he uses exclamation marks to show that he's mad and he means what he says."

"He starts the letter 'Dear Miss No-Good Baby Sister.'"

"I agree with [Cecilia], and in the first line he says 'This is NOT a friendly letter.'"

Continue reading to the end of the book. Ask and briefly discuss:

Q *How does Mike feel about his sister now? What does he do in the letter to show this?*

Students might say:

"Mike is glad to have a sister."

"I agree with [Matt]. He even writes that it's the best thing that could happen to him."

"In addition, he uses capital letters and exclamation points to show how much he wants to wish her a happy birthday."

"He also says he loves her in his closing."

Discuss Purposes for Friendly Letters

Explain that writers of friendly letters keep in mind who they are writing to and why. Ask:

Q *Who is Mike writing to, and why does he write to her?*

Remind the students that last week they wrote letters to you to tell you information about the class. They also wrote letters to their partners and to classmates to tell about themselves and to ask questions, and they wrote a shared letter to a first grade class to give information about the second grade. On a sheet of chart paper entitled "Reasons for Writing a Friendly Letter," write *give information* and *ask questions*. Ask:

Q *What are some other reasons you might want to write a friendly letter to someone?*

List additional reasons on the chart.

Reasons for Writing a Friendly Letter

give information

ask questions

say "hello"

say "get well"

say "thank you"

say you are sorry

invite someone to do something

wish someone a happy birthday or a happy holiday

---

3 Prepare to Write to Family Members

Explain that today the students will each write a friendly letter to a family member. They might write how they feel about that person, as Mike does in *Dear Baby*. They might also write about something that happened to them, or write a special greeting for a birthday, holiday, or other special occasion.

Give the students a moment to decide who they will write to. Then use "Think, Pair, Share" to have partners first think about and then discuss:

 Q *What is the reason you will write to the person you chose?* [pause] *Turn to your partner.*

Q *What is something you might tell that person in your letter?* [pause] *Turn to your partner.*

For each question, have a few volunteers share their thinking with the class. Remind the students to include the five parts of a friendly letter and to use punctuation where needed. They may look at your charted letter from Day 1 for a model. Tell the students that they will share their letters in pairs after writing time.

WRITING TIME

4 ▸ Write Friendly Letters

Distribute lined writing paper. Have the students return to their desks and work silently on their friendly letters for 20–30 minutes.

Join the students in writing for a few minutes, and then confer with individual students.

TEACHER CONFERENCE NOTE

Continue to confer with individual students by having each student read and tell you about her letter. Ask yourself:

* Does the student include all of the parts of a friendly letter?

* Does she tell about herself and ask questions?

* Does she correctly punctuate each part of the letter?

continues

ELL **Note**

Consider having beginning English Language Learners write to their family members in their native language.

> **TEACHER CONFERENCE NOTE** *continued*
>
> Support students by asking them questions such as:
>
> **Q** *Who are you writing to? Why are you writing to [him/her]?*
>
> **Q** *What can you say about yourself in your letter? What questions can you ask?*
>
> **Q** *What punctuation will you use here?*
>
> **Q** *How will you close your letter?*
>
> Document your observations for each student using the "Conference Notes" record sheet (BLM1).

Signal to let the students know when writing time is over.

SHARING AND REFLECTING

▶ **5 Reflect on Audience and Purpose**

Gather the class with partners sitting together, facing you. Ask them to bring their letters with them. Have partners tell each other who they wrote to and why, and then have them read their letters to each other. Alert the students to listen carefully, as they will share something their partner wrote with the class.

Ask and briefly discuss:

Q *Who did your partner write to? What was something your partner said in his or her letter?*

Q *How did you know that you had your partner's full attention when you read your letter?*

Have the students put their letters in their writing folders and explain that they will continue to work on them tomorrow.

Teacher Note

Display the "Reasons for Writing a Friendly Letter" chart for the students to refer to throughout the unit.

EXTENSION

Write Friendly Letters for Other Purposes

Show and discuss examples of other types of friendly letters, such as thank you notes and invitations. Have the students write one or more of these.

Day 3

Materials

- Transparencies of "Unpunctuated Letter 1" and "Unpunctuated Letter 2" (BLM4–BLM5)
- Overhead pen

Exploring Letter Writing

In this lesson, the students:

- Read their writing aloud and listen for periods
- Proofread for punctuation and capitalization

GETTING READY TO WRITE

▶ Introduce Listening for Periods

Have the students stay at their desks today. Remind them that this week they have been exploring how to punctuate a letter. Explain that today they will practice punctuating some sample letters, and then they will check the punctuation of the letter they wrote to a family member yesterday.

Show the letter on the "Unpunctuated Letter 1" transparency. Read it aloud, without pauses. Ask:

Q *What's strange about the way I read this letter?*

Point out that the letter is written as one long sentence and doesn't sound right when read aloud. Ask the students to slowly reread the passage aloud with you and to stop when it feels natural to do so. At each stop (and as appropriate), model writing a period and capitalizing the next letter to begin a new sentence.

Follow this same procedure with the letter on the "Unpunctuated Letter 2" transparency.

WRITING TIME

2 ▶ Complete and Proofread Friendly Letters

Explain that today the students will finish writing the letters they started yesterday, if necessary, and then read them aloud to make sure they have used periods (or question marks or exclamation points) at the ends of sentences and capital letters at the beginnings. If they finish, they may write a letter to anyone they choose.

Have the students work silently for 20–30 minutes to finish their letters and check punctuation. Join the students in writing for a few minutes, and then confer with individual students.

TEACHER CONFERENCE NOTE

Continue to confer with individual students by having each student read and tell you about his letter. Ask yourself:

- Does the student include all of the parts of a friendly letter?

- Does he tell about himself and ask questions?

- Does he correctly punctuate each part of the letter?

Support students by asking them questions such as:

Q *Who are you writing to? Why are you writing to [him/her]?*

Q *What can you say about yourself in your letter? What questions can you ask?*

Q *What punctuation will you use here?*

Q *How will you close your letter?*

Document your observations for each student using the "Conference Notes" record sheet (BLM1).

Signal to let the students know when writing time is over.

SHARING AND REFLECTING

 Reflect on Proofreading for Punctuation

Ask and briefly discuss:

Q *What punctuation did you add to or change in your letter today? Read us that part. Why do you need [a period] there?*

Have the students take their cards and letters home to deliver to their intended recipients.

Day 4

Drafting Friendly Letters

In this lesson, the students:

- Hear and discuss friendly letters
- Write friendly letters
- Use writing time responsibly

Materials

- *Love, Lizzie*
- Index card for each student
- *Assessment Resource Book*

GETTING READY TO WRITE

 Read *Love, Lizzie* Aloud

Gather the class with partners sitting together, facing you. Show *Love, Lizzie* and explain that this is another story that is told through friendly letters. Read the title (including the subtitle) and the names of the author and the illustrator aloud. Briefly discuss:

Q *Why do you think there is a comma between the two words in this title? What does the title tell you about this story?*

Beginning with Lizzie's first letter on page 5, read the story aloud, clarifying vocabulary as you read.

> **Suggested Vocabulary**
>
> **privacy:** space to be alone (p. 5)
> **defending:** protecting (p. 9)
> **support:** help and encourage (p. 9)
> **won the regionals:** beat the other teams in the area (p. 13)
> **pinky swear:** link little fingers and promise something (p. 17)

Ask and discuss the following questions, reading aloud excerpts from the letters to help the students recall what they heard:

Q *In this story, Lizzie writes to her mom who is serving in the military far from home. What are some of the things she tells her mom? What does she ask her mom?*

2 ▶ Prepare to Write Friendly Letters

Explain that today the students will begin a letter to someone they don't see every day. Next week they will have time to complete and proofread their letter, and then they will write a final version. Use "Think, Pair, Share" to have partners first think about and then discuss:

 Q *Who is someone you don't see every day that you might write to?* [pause] *Turn to your partner.*

Signal for the students' attention and have a few volunteers share with the class. Have the students think quietly to themselves about the following questions. Pause between each question to give the students time to think.

Q *What are some things you want this person to know about you?*

Q *What are some things you want to find out about this person?*

After a moment, have partners turn and talk about their thinking.

Encourage the students to use some of the ideas they discussed when they write their letters.

Teacher Note ▶

You might need to help the students choose a recipient for their letter that they don't see or talk with frequently. If the students are struggling to choose someone, you might ask them to think about:

Q *What relatives do you have that you don't see very often?*

Q *What friends do you have that live somewhere else?*

Q *What teachers from past years could you write a letter to?*

WRITING TIME

3 ▶ Write Independently

Distribute lined writing paper and ask the students to write on every other line. Have the students return to their seats and work silently on their letters for 20–30 minutes.

Join the students in writing for a few minutes; then circulate and observe.

CLASS ASSESSMENT NOTE

Observe the students and ask yourself:

- Do the students quickly pick a recipient and begin writing?

- Do they use the five parts of a friendly letter?

- Do they correctly punctuate the date, greeting, and closing?

- Are they able to write something about themselves? Write a question? Tell more?

Support students who are struggling by asking questions such as:

Q *Read this sentence aloud. Where does your voice naturally stop? What punctuation mark will you put there?*

Q *What is something you've done recently that you can tell this person about?*

Q *What would you like to know about this person?*

Record your observations in the *Assessment Resource Book*.

Signal to let the students know when writing time is over.

SHARING AND REFLECTING

4▶ Reflect on Independent Writing

Ask and briefly discuss:

Q *Who did you write to today? What was your reason for writing to this person?*

Q *What punctuation did you use today? Read us a sentence where you used [a comma]. Why did you need [a comma] there?*

Q *How did you work responsibly today?*

Discuss Getting Addresses for Their Letters

Explain that next week the students will complete their drafts, proofread them, and write final versions of their letters. Tell them that at the end of the week they will learn how to address envelopes for their letters. To do this, they will each need to bring in the address of the person they are writing to. Discuss:

Q *How will you get the address you need?*

> **Students might say:**
>
> "I'll ask my mom."
>
> "I have a letter from my grandmother with her address."
>
> "I'll look in our address book."

Hand out the index cards. Explain that each student will bring an index card home, write the address on it, and then bring it back to school. Model writing a name and address where everyone can see it, pointing out the house or building number, street name, town or city, state, zip code, and any other features of the address. Then have the students put their letters in their writing folders and their index cards where they will remember to take them home.

Week 3 Overview

UNIT 5: LETTER WRITING

Writing Focus

- Students proofread for punctuation and spelling.

- Students write final versions of their friendly letters.

- Students address envelopes.

- Students share their letters from the Author's Chair.

Social Focus

- Students make decisions and solve problems respectfully.

- Students reflect on their relationships to others.

- Students express interest in and appreciation for one another's writing.

DO AHEAD

- Prior to Day 1, make a transparency of the letter to Mrs. Hartwell (BLM6).

- (Optional) Prior to Day 2, collect stationery for the students to use when writing the final versions of their friendly letters.

TEACHER AS WRITER

"If doubtful whether to end with 'yours faithfully,' or 'yours truly,' or 'yours most truly,' (there are at least a dozen varieties, before you reach 'yours affectionately'), refer to your correspondent's last letter, and make your winding-up at least as friendly as his: in fact, even if a shade more friendly, it will do no harm!"

— Lewis Carroll

Write a friendly letter in response to a letter, card, or e-mail that you have received. As you did last week, think about what you would like this person to know about your life, and ask questions about what you would like to know about his or her life.

Day 1

Materials

- *First Year Letters*
- *Student Writing Handbook* page 16
- Transparency of the letter to Mrs. Hartwell (BLM6)
- *Assessment Resource Book*

Informal Proofreading

In this lesson, the students:

- Practice proofreading a letter
- Reach agreement and make decisions
- Complete and proofread their draft letters

GETTING READY TO WRITE

1 ▶ Briefly Discuss Addresses

Have partners get their writing folders, index cards with addresses, and *Student Writing Handbooks* and sit together at desks today. Remind them that last week they each began writing a letter to someone they do not see very often. Ask:

Q *Who remembered to bring an address for their letter? Where does the person you are writing to live?*

Direct the students who brought in an address to put it in their writing folder for safekeeping, and remind the other students that they are responsible for bringing in an address for their letter.

2 ▶ Practice Proofreading a Letter

Remind the students that last week they learned how to punctuate a letter. Show *First Year Letters* and remind the students that this book includes letters from students to the teacher. Show page 4 and review that this is the first letter that Josh wrote to Mrs. Hartwell. Explain that since it was the beginning of the year, the class had not yet learned how to punctuate a letter.

Ask the students to turn to the copy of the letter on *Student Writing Handbook* page 16 as you show the transparency of the letter on the overhead projector. Ask the students to follow along as you read the letter aloud. Then ask:

Q *What punctuation do we need to add to the [greeting/body of the letter/closing], and why? Turn to your partner.*

Have volunteers share their ideas, and use their suggestions to make corrections on the transparency. As you make corrections, have the students make the same corrections in their own handbooks. Follow this same procedure for the next two questions:

Q *What would you add to how Josh wrote the date? Turn to your partner.*

Q *What spelling errors has Josh made that need correction? Turn to your partner.*

Again, have volunteers share their ideas, and use their suggestions to make corrections on the transparency. If necessary, be ready to point out and correct any punctuation, capitalization, or spelling errors that the students overlook.

Explain that the students will use what they have learned about proofreading to proofread their own letters today. Remind them that the first place they should go to check the spelling of a word is the word bank in their *Student Writing Handbooks*. Have the students turn to this section in their handbooks; then ask:

Q *If a word you're looking for does not appear in the word bank, what will you do to check the correct spelling?*

Students might say:

"I could ask my partner or someone at my table if they know how to spell it."

"I could look it up online."

"I could look on the word wall."

"If I know where I read that word in a book, I can go look it up there."

"I could look it up in a dictionary."

Encourage the students to use the strategies they suggested as they proofread today.

◀ **Teacher Note**

To provide your students with further practice in punctuation, capitalization, and other skills and conventions of written English, schedule time to do the appropriate activities in the *Skill Practice Teaching Guide* with them.

WRITING TIME

3 ▶ Complete and Proofread Drafts

Have the students work silently for 15–20 minutes to complete and proofread their drafts. As they work, circulate and observe them.

> ### CLASS ASSESSMENT NOTE
>
> Observe the students and ask yourself:
>
> - Do the students use the five parts of a friendly letter?
> - Do they notice and correct incorrect or missing capitalization or punctuation?
> - Do they notice and correct misspelled words?
>
> Support students who are struggling by asking questions such as:
>
> **Q** *Read this sentence aloud. Where does your voice naturally stop? What punctuation mark will you put there?*
>
> Record your observations in the *Assessment Resource Book*.

SHARING AND REFLECTING

4 ▶ Reflect on Proofreading for Punctuation and Spelling

Ask and briefly discuss:

Q *What punctuation did you change or add in your draft today? Read us a sentence in which you changed something. Why did you need [a period] there?*

Q *What words did you check the spelling of today? What words did you find in your word bank? How did you check on words that were not in the word bank?*

Explain that tomorrow the students will write final versions of their letters. Remind the students that they are each responsible for bringing in the address for their letter if they have not already done so.

Day 2

Writing Final Versions

In this lesson, the students:

* Write final versions of their letters
* Imagine and discuss how others might feel
* Share friendly sentences from their letters
* Express interest in one another's writing

GETTING READY TO WRITE

1 ▶ Briefly Discuss Addresses

Have the students stay at their desks today. Remind them that they are writing a letter to someone they do not see very often. Ask:

Q *Who remembered to bring in an address for the letter? Where does the person you are writing to live?*

Direct the students who brought in an address to put it in their writing folder for safekeeping. Explain that the students who have not yet brought in an address need to do so by tomorrow, as they will be addressing envelopes for their letters then.

Explain that today the students will write the final versions of their letters. Show students the paper (or stationery) they will use and explain that they should use their best handwriting when writing their final versions.

Materials

* (Optional) Stationery (see "Do Ahead" on page 445)

WRITING TIME

 Write Final Versions

Distribute lined writing paper (or stationery) and have the students work silently on the final versions of their letters for 20–30 minutes. As they work, circulate, observe, and offer assistance.

Signal to let the students know when writing time is over.

Teacher Note ▶

Some of your students may still be completing or proofreading their drafts. Help these students complete these steps so they can move to writing their final versions as soon as possible.

SHARING AND REFLECTING

3 **Share Sentences and Reflect on How Others Might Feel**

Have the students think quietly to themselves for a moment about:

Q *How do you want the person you are writing to to feel when he or she reads your letter? What friendly words did you include in your letter to help him or her feel [good]?*

Explain that you would like each student to choose one sentence from his letter that he feels is friendly, or that he thinks will make the recipient feel good, to read aloud to the class. Give the students a moment to choose their sentences, and then go around the room and have each student read her sentence aloud, without comment.

When all of the students have read, ask and briefly discuss:

Q *What did you hear that makes you want to know more about someone's letter?*

Explain that the students will have time to finish their final versions tomorrow, if they haven't already. Have the students put their letters in their writing folders. Explain that they will put their letters in envelopes tomorrow and address them. Remind the students who have not yet brought in an address for their letter to do so by tomorrow.

Day 3

Publishing

In this lesson, the students:

- Address envelopes for their letters
- Present their letters from the Author's Chair
- Express interest in and appreciation for one another's writing

GETTING READY TO WRITE

1 Discuss How to Address an Envelope

Have the students begin the lesson at their desks. Have them take out their writing folders, their index cards with addresses, and their *Student Writing Handbooks*. Explain that today they will each address an envelope for their letter. Tell the students that the United States Postal Service delivers more than 200 billion pieces of mail every year. Ask:

Q *Why is it important to learn how to address an envelope correctly? What might happen if we don't address envelopes correctly?*

Have the students turn to *Student Writing Handbook* page 17. Explain that the envelope pictured there is correctly addressed. Point out that the address of the person sending the letter is written in the upper left-hand corner, while the address of the person receiving the letter goes in the middle of the envelope. Point out that an address to someone in the United States includes the person's name, street address, town, state, and zip code. Ask and briefly discuss:

Q *Why do you think the sender's name and address need to be on the envelope?*

Materials

- Addresses for letters, brought by students from home
- *Student Writing Handbook* page 17
- Envelope for each student
- Author's Chair

◀ **Teacher Note**

If you have students who are writing to people outside the United States, explain that you will help them individually to address their envelopes.

Direct the students' attention to the blank envelope that appears below the other envelope on *Student Writing Handbook* page 17. State that the students will practice addressing an envelope using this blank envelope. First, they will write their own name and address on the lines for the sender's address. Then, using the index card with the address they brought from home, they will write the recipient's name and address on the lines in the center of the envelope. After practicing once in their handbooks, the students will address their own envelopes.

WRITING TIME

 Address Envelopes

Have the students practice addressing the envelope in their handbooks. As they finish, distribute an envelope to each student and have the students work on addressing the envelopes. Have them work silently for 15–20 minutes. As they work, circulate, observe, and offer assistance.

Signal to let the students know when writing time is over. Have them take their letters out of their writing folders. Show them how to fold their letters to fit in their envelopes and have them do so. Tell them that they will *not* seal the envelopes yet, as they will be sharing their letters with the class from the Author's Chair.

SHARING AND REFLECTING

Share Letters from the Author's Chair

Gather the class with partners sitting together, facing the Author's Chair. Have them bring their letters (in their envelopes) with them.

Explain that each student will show and read her envelope and letter aloud to the class. Remind the authors to speak in a loud, clear voice, and remind the audience to show interest in and appreciation for their classmates' writing.

Teacher Note ▶

Addressing an envelope may be challenging for some students. Be ready to assist as necessary. If you have students who are still writing their final drafts, offer them extra support, if necessary, so they can move to addressing their envelopes as soon as possible.

Call on a student to come to the Author's Chair and read her envelope and letter aloud. After the author has read, facilitate a discussion, asking questions such as:

Q *What did you learn about [Juanita] from [her] letter?*

Q *How would you feel if you received this letter? What words did [Juanita] use that would make you feel that way?*

Follow this procedure to have other students share from the Author's Chair.

4 ▶ Reflect on Audience Behavior During Author's Chair Sharing

Ask and briefly discuss:

Q *What did we do well as an audience today? What do we want to work on the next time authors share their work?*

Q *If you shared today, how did the audience make you feel? What did they do that made you feel [relaxed/nervous/proud]?*

Ask the students to put their letters (in their envelopes) in their writing folders. Assure the students who haven't yet shared that they will have a chance to share their letters from the Author's Chair tomorrow.

Day 4

Materials

- Author's Chair

Publishing

In this lesson, the students:

- Review and reflect on writing letters
- List other people they might want to write to
- Present their letters from the Author's Chair
- Express interest in and appreciation for one another's writing
- Write freely

GETTING READY TO SHARE

1 Review and Reflect on Writing Letters

Gather the class with partners sitting together, facing the Author's Chair. Have them bring their writing notebooks and pencils with them. Also have the students who have not yet shared their letters bring their letters with them.

Review that during the past three weeks the class has explored letter writing and written many letters. Ask and briefly discuss:

 Q *What have you learned about writing a friendly letter? Turn to your partner.*

Signal for the students' attention and have a few volunteers share with the class.

> **Students might say:**
>
> "I learned that in a friendly letter you tell about yourself."
>
> "In addition to what [Gemma] said, I learned that you can ask questions in your letter."
>
> "I learned that a friendly letter has five parts."
>
> "I learned how to address an envelope for my letter."

FACILITATION TIP

Reflect on your experience with **pacing class discussions** during this unit. Do the pacing techniques feel comfortable and natural to you? Do you find yourself using them throughout the school day? What effect has your focus on pacing had on your students' participation in discussions? We encourage you to continue to think about how to pace class discussions throughout the year.

2 ▶ List Other People They Might Want to Write To

Explain that, now that the students know how to write a friendly letter, they may write one anytime to anyone they know. Use "Think, Pair, Share" to have partners first think about and then discuss:

 Q *Who else might you want to write a friendly letter to?* [pause] *Turn to your partner.*

Have the students open their writing notebooks to their writing ideas section, label the next blank page "People to Write To," and list the names of people they might want to write to in the future.

After a few moments, signal for the students' attention and have a few volunteers share what they wrote with the class. Encourage the students to remember their list and to continue to write letters during free writing time or on their own.

Have the students set their notebooks and pencils aside for Author's Chair sharing.

SHARING AND REFLECTING

3 ▶ Share Letters from the Author's Chair

Remind the authors to speak in a loud, clear voice, and remind the audience to show interest in and appreciation for their classmates' writing.

Call on a student to come to the Author's Chair and read his envelope and letter aloud. After the author has read, facilitate a discussion by asking questions such as:

Q *What did you learn about [Jamal] from [his] letter?*

Q *How would you feel if you received this letter? What words did [Jamal] use that would make you feel that way?*

Follow this procedure to have other students share from the Author's Chair.

Teacher Note

If necessary, continue Author's Chair sharing on another day so ◀ that all of the students have a chance to share their letters with the class.

Teacher Note

Once the students have shared their letters from the Author's Chair, explain that they are free to seal the envelopes and mail their letters. Tell the students that they can ask a parent or other adult to help them attach postage and locate a mailbox or post office. (Alternately, you might wish to mail the letters together as a class, as described in the Extension.)

▶4 **Reflect on Audience Behavior During Author's Chair Sharing**

Ask and briefly discuss:

Q *What did we do well as an audience today? What do we want to work on the next time authors share their work?*

Q *If you shared today, how did the audience make you feel? What did they do that made you feel [relaxed/nervous/proud]?*

FREE WRITING TIME

▶5 **Write Freely**

Explain that the students will now have time to write freely. They may write another friendly letter to someone on their "People to Write To" list or they may write about anything they choose. Ask and briefly discuss:

 Q *Who might you write to, or what might you write about? Turn to your partner.*

Teacher Note

This is the last week of the unit. You will need to reassign partners before beginning the next unit.

Have the students write freely for 10–15 minutes.

EXTENSION

Mail the Letters

Consider planning a trip to the local post office to mail the students' letters and to take a tour. Prior to the trip, read about how the mail is processed. Some possible read-aloud books include *The Post Office Book* by Gail Gibbons, *How It Happens at the Post Office* by Dawn Frederick, and *Sending a Letter* by Alex Stewart; the latter includes a history of how sending a letter has changed through time.

If a trip to the post office is not feasible, then have the class walk to a mailbox to mail the letters. (Remember to put stamps on the letters before mailing them.)

Poems and Words

Unit 6 Poems and Words

During this three-week unit, the students hear and discuss poems, and write poems on assigned topics and topics they choose. They explore descriptive language in poems, informally explore figurative language, and generate lists of interesting words to use in their own poems. They share their poems in pairs and with the class, and each proofread and revise a poem for publication in a class collection of poetry. Socially, they ask one another questions about their writing, explain their thinking, listen to one another and build on one another's thinking, and express interest in and appreciation for one another's writing.

Development Across the Grades

Grade	Elements of Poetry	Language and Craft	Skills and Conventions
2	• Using descriptive language (words that describe how things look, sound, and move) to write poems • Writing poems about topics of interest	• Exploring figurative language • Generating lists of descriptive words	• Using the word bank
3	*(There is no poetry unit in the core program at grade 3. However, a supplemental Grade 3 Poetry Genre unit is available separately.)*		
4	• Creating images using sensory details • Using sound and typography (or shape) in poems to support their meaning	• Simile • Personification • Onomatopoeia, repetition, and alliteration • Rhythm and rhyme	• Exploring how poets follow or intentionally break punctuation rules for poetic effect
5	• Creating images using sensory details • Using sounds and poetic forms to support meaning	• Metaphor, simile • Personification • Rhythm, rhyme, and repetition • Line length	• Exploring how poets follow or intentionally break punctuation rules for poetic effect

UNIT OVERVIEW

WEEK	DAY 1	DAY 2	DAY 3	DAY 4
1	**Exploring Poems:** "Tree House," "Boa Constrictor" **Focus:** • Discussing interesting words in poems	**Exploring Poems:** "The Coyote," "The Tiger" **Focus:** • Listing words about animals • Writing animal poems	**Exploring Poems:** "Knoxville, Tennessee" **Focus:** • Listing words about summer • Writing poems about summer	**Exploring Poems:** "Lettuce," "Peaches" **Focus:** • Listing words about food • Writing poems about food
2	**Exploring Poems:** "My Baby Brother" **Focus:** • Writing a shared poem about the class clock • Listing words that describe how things look • Writing poems about classroom objects	**Exploring Poems:** "Wind Song" **Focus:** • Listening for and listing school sounds • Writing a shared poem about school sounds	**Exploring Poems:** "Weather" **Focus:** • Discussing and listing sound words • Writing poems using sound words	**Exploring Poems:** "Fish" **Focus:** • Discussing and listing movement words • Writing poems using movement words
3	**Exploring Poems:** "Clouds," "Rain Poem" **Focus:** • Exploring figurative language • Writing poems about rain	**Exploring Poems:** "The Steam Shovel" **Focus:** • Exploring figurative language • Writing poems on topics they choose	**Proofreading and Writing Final Versions** **Focus:** • Choosing poems to publish • Revising and proofreading poems • Writing final versions	**Publishing** **Focus:** • Sharing poems from the Author's Chair • Expressing interest in and appreciation for one another's writing • Writing freely

Overview

UNIT 6: POEMS AND WORDS

Poetry

"Tree House" and **"Boa Constrictor"**
by Shel Silverstein
(see pages 482–483)

A poet uses humor and descriptive language to stimulate the imagination.

"The Coyote" and **"The Tiger"**
by Douglas Florian
(see pages 484–485)

Coyotes howl and tigers *purrrr* in these two animal poems.

"Knoxville, Tennessee"
by Nikki Giovanni
(see page 486)

A poet explains why she likes summer best.

"Lettuce" and **"Peaches"**
by Alma Flor Ada, English translation by Rosa Zubizarreta
(see pages 487–488)

These poems help readers imagine they are holding crinkly lettuce and golden peaches.

Writing Focus

- Students hear, visualize, read, and discuss poems.

- Students explore interesting and descriptive words in poems.

- Students generate word lists and writing ideas.

- Students write poems.

Social Focus

- Students listen respectfully to the thinking of others and share their own.

- Students express interest in and appreciation for one another's writing.

- Students build on one another's thinking.

DO AHEAD

- Prior to Day 1, decide how you will randomly assign partners to work together during this unit. See the front matter in volume 1 for suggestions about assigning partners randomly (page xiii) and for considerations for pairing English Language Learners (page xxvii).

- Prior to Day 1, review some of the poems and chants the students have learned this year. If your students have not heard much poetry this year, consider taking time to immerse them in poetry before you proceed with this unit. Read poems aloud, act them out, and move and clap to their rhythms. To find poems online, search using the keywords "children's poems."

- Preview and discuss this week's poems with your English Language Learners. If possible, show them related illustrations, objects, or photographs (such as pictures of lettuce and peaches) to aid their comprehension.

TEACHER AS WRITER

"Poetry is language at its most distilled and most powerful."
— Rita Dove

This week, seek out poems that inspire you. Websites offering wide selections of poems include the Academy of American Poets website (www.poets.org), *Poetry* magazine's website (www.poetryfoundation.org), and Poetry Daily (www.poems.com). You might also search online using the keyword "poems."

Keep in mind that it is not necessary to completely understand a poem in order to appreciate something about it. Choose a few poems you especially enjoy and copy or paste them into your writing notebook. Jot down what you like about them—word choices, figurative language (such as similes, metaphors, and personification), the length or shape of the poems, or anything else you notice.

Day 1

Materials

- "Tree House" (see page 482)
- "Boa Constrictor" (see page 483)
- *Student Writing Handbook* pages 18–19

Exploring Poems

In this lesson, the students:

- Work with a new partner
- Hear, read, and discuss poems
- Explore interesting words in poems
- Share their partner's writing with the class

About Writing Poems in Grade 2

The primary focus of this unit is to expand the students' writing vocabularies by introducing them to the vivid language of poetry. The students discuss words they hear in poems, generate lists of interesting words, and use those words as they write poems. They hear and discuss poems that contain such poetic elements as rhyme, rhythm, repetition, and figurative language, preparing them for further study of these elements of poetry in later grades.

As you read aloud and discuss poems, write shared poems, and support your students' writing, adopt a relaxed attitude and keep the focus on word play and fun. Also, listen carefully to your students during discussions and during the writing of shared poems; children have a natural affinity for the inventive, musical language of poetry.

GETTING READY TO WRITE

Teacher Note

The partners you assign today will stay together for the entire unit, as well as for Unit 7.

Making Meaning® Teacher

You can either have the students work with their current *Making Meaning* partner or assign a different partner for the writing lessons.

1 ▶ Assign New Partners and Introduce Poetry

Randomly assign partners (see "Do Ahead" on page 461). Gather the class with partners sitting together, facing you. Have them bring their *Student Writing Handbooks* with them.

Signal for the students' attention and remind them that this year they have written fiction, nonfiction, and letters. Explain that during the next few weeks they will explore another kind of writing—poetry.

Briefly mention some of the poems, chants, or rhymes the students have heard this year. Ask and briefly discuss:

Q *What do you think a poem is?*

Q *How do you think a poem is different from a story?*

> **Students might say:**
>
> "I think poems rhyme."
>
> "I agree and disagree with [Jacob]. Some poems rhyme and some don't."
>
> "Poems are short. Stories are long."
>
> "I agree with [Ricca]. A poem is usually on one page. A story can be so long that it has chapters."

Explain that in the coming days the students will hear many poems and try writing poems themselves. Tell them that you will read two poems aloud today. Invite the students to listen for how the words in the poems help them make pictures in their minds.

2 Read and Discuss "Tree House"

Ask the students to close their eyes and make a picture in their minds as they listen to a poem by Shel Silverstein called "Tree House." Read the poem aloud twice slowly and clearly.

> **ELL Vocabulary**
>
> English Language Learners may benefit from discussing the following vocabulary:
>
> **cozy:** comfortable and warm
>
> **neat:** clean

Ask and briefly discuss:

Q *What kind of place is the tree house?*

Q *What does the poet mean by a "street house"?*

Teacher Note

At this point, the students will likely have a limited understanding of what makes a poem a poem. Just have them share their ideas without comment. They will gain a better understanding of poems as they hear and discuss them in this unit.

 Note

Prior to reading the poem, explain that a tree house is a playhouse built in a tree. If possible, show a picture of a tree house. Facilitate a class discussion about tree houses by asking questions such as:

Q *Have you ever seen a tree house? Tell us about it.*

Q *What might you do in a tree house?*

Students might say:

"The tree house is a secret place in the trees."

"In addition to what [Aileen] said, it is cozy."

"I think a street house is a regular house on the street."

Have the students open to *Student Writing Handbook* page 18, where "Tree House" is reproduced. Ask them to follow along as you reread the poem, and invite them to look for words that describe the tree house. Read the poem aloud again, and then ask:

 Q *What words does the poet use to describe the tree house? Turn to your partner.*

Signal for the students' attention and have a few volunteers share with the class. Follow up with questions such as:

Q *What do you think Shel Silverstein means by "a secret you and me house"?*

Q *Why do you think he calls his tree house a "free house"?*

Students might say:

"He means 'it's a special place for the two of us.'"

"Maybe he says it is secret because you can't see it in the branches."

"It's a 'free house' because you can be yourself and not worry about things like wiping your feet."

 Read and Discuss "Boa Constrictor"

Have the students close their eyes and tell them that you will read another poem by Shel Silverstein, called "Boa Constrictor." Explain that a boa constrictor is a large snake that winds itself around its prey. Read the poem aloud twice, slowly and clearly, clarifying vocabulary on the first reading.

Suggested Vocabulary

dread: fear

Ask and briefly discuss:

Q *What's funny about the poem?*

Have the students open to *Student Writing Handbook* page 19, where "Boa Constrictor" is reproduced. Ask them to follow along as you reread the poem, and invite them to look for funny words or words that they like. Read the poem aloud again, and then ask:

Q *Which words do you like or do you think are funny? Turn to your partner.*

Signal for the students' attention and have a few volunteers share with the class.

> **Students might say:**
>
> "I like the long word at the end. It's not really a word. It's a noise."
>
> "I like 'I don't like it—one bit' because it's a funny thing to say if a snake is eating you."
>
> "I like the parts that rhyme—like 'Oh, gee,/It's up to my knee.'"

Point out that poets often have fun with words by repeating them, using them in funny ways, or sometimes just making them up.

4 ▶ Discuss How Poems Look

Have the students look at "Tree House" and "Boa Constrictor" again and think about how they look on the page. Discuss:

Q *How do these poems look different from stories?*

> **Students might say:**
>
> "The words go down the page."
>
> "The lines are short. Some have only two words."
>
> "The poems are short. Stories are longer."

Point out that poets often write short lines, rather than writing all the way across the page like authors of stories do. Encourage the students to keep in mind how poems look as they write their own poems this week.

WRITING TIME

5 ▶ **Write Independently**

Explain that during writing time today the students may try writing a poem or they may write about anything else they choose. They might write about a special place like a tree house or an unusual animal like a boa constrictor. Ask and briefly discuss:

 Q *What is something you might write about today? Turn to your partner.*

Signal for the students' attention and have a few volunteers share with the class. Have the students return to desks with partners sitting together. Then have them open their writing notebooks to the next blank page and write silently for 20–30 minutes.

Join the students in writing for a few minutes, and then circulate and observe.

Signal to let the students know when writing time is over.

Teacher Note ▶

Note that today the students may write poems or anything else they choose. On Day 2, after exposure to two more poems, all of the students will be asked to try writing a poem.

SHARING AND REFLECTING

6 ▶ **Share Writing and Reflect**

Explain that partners will read their poems to each other and then each tell the class an interesting word their partner wrote. Have partners share their poems with each other. After they have had time to share, signal for their attention and ask:

Q *What did your partner write about today?*

Q *What is an interesting word your partner wrote?*

For each question, have a few volunteers share their thinking with the class. Explain that tomorrow the students will explore more poems.

EXTENSIONS

Explore Rhythm in "Tree House"

As a class, read "Tree House" aloud, clapping on each stressed syllable of the poem (for example, "A *tree* house, a *free* house,/A *se*cret you and *me* house").

Read More Poems

Throughout the unit, find other times of the day to expose the students to poetry. Have the students act out poems, clap out their rhythms, and close their eyes to visualize them. Discuss the language the poets use to describe how things look, sound, or move.

Day 2

Materials

- "The Coyote" (see page 484)
- "The Tiger" (see page 485)
- *Student Writing Handbook* pages 20–21
- Chart paper (both lined and unlined) and a marker

Exploring Poems

In this lesson, the students:

- Visualize poems
- Generate and list words about animals
- Write animal poems that begin with "I am a _____"
- Express interest in and appreciation for one another's writing

GETTING READY TO WRITE

▶ 1 Read and Visualize "The Coyote"

Gather the class with partners sitting together, facing you. Have them bring their *Student Writing Handbooks* with them. Remind the students that yesterday they heard and talked about two poems by Shel Silverstein, "Tree House" and "Boa Constrictor." Explain that today they will hear two poems by a different poet, Douglas Florian.

Ask the students to close their eyes and make a picture in their minds as they listen to the first poem. Read "The Coyote" aloud twice, slowly and clearly, clarifying vocabulary on the first reading.

> **Suggested Vocabulary**
>
> **prowl:** move around secretly to hunt

Have the students open to *Student Writing Handbook* page 20, where "The Coyote" is reproduced. Ask them to follow along as you reread the poem aloud; then ask and briefly discuss:

Q *What do you imagine when you read this poem?*

Q *Why do you think the poet chose to write the word* coyote *the way he did?*

Students might say:

"Some of the words rhyme and some don't."

"Many of the words have a growly sound."

"He wrote the word *coyote* so it looks like the sound a coyote makes."

 2 Read and Visualize "The Tiger"

Ask the students to close their eyes and make a picture in their minds as they listen to the second poem. Read "The Tiger" aloud twice, slowly and clearly, clarifying vocabulary on the first reading.

> **Suggested Vocabulary**
>
> **blurrrr:** (blur) something that is hard to see clearly because it is moving so fast
>
> **ELL Vocabulary**
>
> English Language Learners may benefit from discussing additional vocabulary, including:
>
> **purrrr:** (purr) soft rumbling noise a cat makes when it is happy
> **furrrr:** (fur) hair on an animal
> **speed:** go very fast
> **hunt:** look for animals to kill and eat

Ask:

 Q *What did you see in your mind? Turn to your partner.*

Signal for the students' attention and have a few volunteers share their visualizations with the class. As they share, reread the words from the poem that helped them make their mental pictures.

Have the students open to *Student Writing Handbook* page 21, where "The Tiger" is reproduced. Invite them to read the poem aloud with you, emphasizing the "rrrr" sounds. Ask:

Q *Why do you think Douglas Florian wrote the poem in this way?*

Teacher Note

If you notice partners struggling to describe their mental pictures to each other, signal for the class's attention. Model by rereading the first two lines of the poem, closing your eyes, and thinking aloud about your mental picture and the words in the poem that evoked it. Have the students close their eyes as you read the poem aloud once more. Then have partners discuss what they saw in their minds.

Students might say:

"The way he writes the word *purrrr* helps you hear the sound."

"I agree with [LaTisha]. It's the same for the word *blurrrr*. Adding the extra *r*'s helps you picture that the tiger goes so fast he's hard to see."

"In addition to what [Nathan] said, I think that he put in all the 'rrrr' sounds to make the poem sound like a tiger growling!"

Point out that Douglas Florian, like Shel Silverstein in "Boa Constrictor," uses words in a fun way. Poets commonly repeat words, spell or use words in a funny way, or make up words just to make their poems fun to say and hear.

▶ 3 Generate Words for Animal Poems

Ask:

Q *"The Tiger" begins with the line "I am a cat." What other animals could we write about in a poem that begins with "I am a _____"?*

As the students make suggestions, record their ideas on a sheet of chart paper entitled "I am a _____." Select one of the items on the list, and ask:

Q *Imagine that you are writing a poem that begins with "I am a [monkey]." What words could you include to describe what you look like? Sound like?*

Q *What words might describe how you move? Where you live?*

As the students make suggestions, write a short poem by recording their ideas as lines or short sentences on sheet of lined chart paper (see the diagram). Repeat this activity with another animal from the "I am a _____" chart.

Teacher Note ▶

If the students have difficulty answering these questions, stimulate their thinking by asking follow-up questions such as:

Q *What color are you?*

Q *How big are you?*

Q *What does your [skin/fur] look like?*

Q *What do your ears look like? Your nose? Eyes? Legs? Tail? Teeth?*

I am a _____.

monkey

alligator

lion

wolf

bunny rabbit

puppy

I am a monkey.

I have brown hair.

I have a loopy tail.

Screech! Screech!

I swing through the trees

In the rainforest.

I am an alligator.

I have a long snout

And big, sharp teeth.

I have bumps all over.

My home is the swamp.

Explain that today each student will choose an animal and write an "I am a _____" poem. Encourage the students to include words that describe what the animal looks and sounds like, how it moves, and where it lives.

WRITING TIME

4▶ Write Animal Poems

Teacher Note ▶

Students may or may not write pieces that look like actual poems. This is to be expected, as poetry is a challenging form to learn to write. At this point, accept all of their efforts to write about animals using the "I am a _____" prompt, and encourage them to include descriptive words about where the animals live and how the animals look, sound, and move.

Have the students return to their seats and each work silently on an "I am a _____" poem for 10–15 minutes.

Join the students in writing for a few minutes, and then circulate and observe.

Signal to let the students know when writing time is over.

SHARING AND REFLECTING

5▶ Share Poems and Reflect

Teacher Note ▶

You might say, "I noticed that [Marie] used the word *buzzzzz* to tell how a bee sounds. That's a fun word to say and hear, and it helps us picture in our minds how the bee sounds. Let's say that word together."

Have a few volunteers read their poems to the class. After each student shares, point out one or two interesting words the student used in the poem.

Invite the students to comment on the poems by asking:

Q *How did [Marie] describe herself as a [bee]?*

Q *What words in [Marie's] poem did you like? Why?*

Explain that tomorrow the students will have a chance to write more poems.

Day 3

Exploring Poems

In this lesson, the students:

- Hear, read, and discuss a poem
- Generate and list words about summer
- Write poems about summer
- Get ideas by listening to one another
- Express interest in and appreciation for one another's writing

GETTING READY TO WRITE

1 ### Read and Discuss "Knoxville, Tennessee"

Gather the class with partners sitting together, facing you. Have the students bring their *Student Writing Handbooks* with them. Explain that today they will hear the poem "Knoxville, Tennessee," by Nikki Giovanni. Explain that Nikki Giovanni grew up in the city of Knoxville in the state of Tennessee, and that in this poem she tells what she likes about summertime in Knoxville.

Read the poem aloud twice, slowly and clearly, clarifying vocabulary during the first reading.

Suggested Vocabulary

okra and greens: kinds of vegetables

buttermilk: liquid that is left over after butter has been churned from cream

gospel music: a type of music that is sung in some churches

ELL Vocabulary

English Language Learners may benefit from discussing additional vocabulary, including:

barbecue: food cooked outdoors over an open fire

barefooted: not wearing shoes or socks

Materials

- "Knoxville, Tennessee" (see page 486)
- *Student Writing Handbook* pages 22–23
- Chart paper and a marker

◀ **Teacher Note**

You might point out that "Knoxville, Tennessee" is an example of a poem that does not rhyme, and that non-rhyming poems are called *free verse*.

Ask the students to open to *Student Writing Handbook* pages 22–23, where "Knoxville, Tennessee" is reproduced. Have them follow along as you reread the first stanza aloud; then ask:

 Q *What foods does the poet like to eat in the summer? Turn to your partner.*

Signal for the students' attention and have the students follow along as you reread the second stanza aloud; then ask:

 Q *What does the poet like to do in the summer? Turn to your partner.*

Signal for the students' attention and point out that the poet includes many details about what she likes to eat and do during the summer. These details help the reader get a clearer picture of what summer was like for her.

▶2 Generate Words for Poems About Summer

Explain that today the students will write poems about what they like about summer. Ask the students to close their eyes and think quietly to themselves as you ask the following questions. Pause between each question to give the students time to think.

Q *What do you like to do for fun in the summer?*

Q *Where do you like to go?*

Q *What do you like to eat and drink?*

Have the students open their eyes and briefly share their thinking with their partner.

Signal for the students' attention and repeat each question one at a time. After each question, have a few volunteers share their ideas with the class. Record the ideas as single words or phrases on a sheet of chart paper entitled "Summer Words."

Summer Words

swim at the park

ride my bike

go swimming with my dog

my grandmother's house

baseball games

chocolate ice cream

watermelon

cold lemonade

hot dogs

---

3 Think About First Lines

Point out that Nikki Giovanni begins "Knoxville, Tennessee" with the words *I always like summer/best.* Tell the students that they can begin their own poems with those words or with any other words they choose. Ask:

Q *What other words might you write to start your poem about summer?*

Students might say:

"I might write, *I love summer.*"

"I'll start with, *Here's what I like about summer.*"

"I'll say, *I can't wait for summer.*"

Remind the students that during writing time today they will each write a poem about what they like about summer. Encourage them to use the ideas on the "Summer Words" chart and any other interesting words they think of in their poem.

◀ **Teacher Note**

If the students struggle to suggest ideas, stimulate their thinking by suggesting some ideas like those in the "Students might say" note.

WRITING TIME

4▸ Write Poems About Summer

Have the students return to their seats and work silently on poems about summer for 20–30 minutes. Join the students in writing for a few minutes, and then circulate and observe.

Signal to let the students know when writing time is over.

REFLECTING AND SHARING

5▸ Share Poems and Reflect on Getting Ideas

Have a few volunteers read their poems to the class. After each student shares, point out something you liked about the poem, and then invite the class to comment on the poem by asking questions such as:

Q *What did you like about [Michael's] poem?*

Q *What words did you hear that helped you make pictures in your mind?*

Q *What ideas did you get for your own writing by listening to [Michael's] poem?*

Explain that tomorrow the students will hear and write more poems.

FACILITATION TIP

During this unit, we encourage you to **avoid repeating or paraphrasing** students' responses. Is it easy to habitually repeat what students say when they speak too softly, or to paraphrase them when they don't speak clearly. This teaches the students to listen to you but not necessarily to one another. Try to refrain from repeating or paraphrasing and see what happens. Encourage the students to take responsibility by asking one another to speak up or by asking a question if they don't understand what a classmate has said. (See the front matter in volume 1 for special considerations for English Language Learners.)

Teacher Note

Display the "Summer Words" chart for the students to refer to throughout the unit.

Day 4

Exploring Poems

In this lesson, the students:

- Hear, read, and discuss poems
- Explore interesting words in poems
- Generate and list words about food
- Write poems about food
- Get ideas by listening to one another

GETTING READY TO WRITE

1 Read and Discuss "Lettuce"

Gather the class with partners sitting together, facing you. Have the students bring their *Student Writing Handbooks* with them.

Explain that today the students will hear two poems by Alma Flor Ada from a collection of poems she has written about the lives of farmworkers who work in fields picking fruits and vegetables.

Read "Lettuce" aloud twice; then ask and briefly discuss:

Q *What is happening in the poem? Why do you think that?*

> **Students might say:**
>
> "The workers are picking lettuce. It says there is lettuce in the field."
>
> "They're filling boxes with lettuce. It says the empty boxes are waiting for them."
>
> "They are working hard. They have to bend their backs."

Have the students open to *Student Writing Handbook* page 24, where "Lettuce" is reproduced. Ask them to follow along as you read the poem again; then ask:

 Q *What words does the poet use to help us imagine the lettuce? Turn to your partner.*

Materials

- "Lettuce" (see page 487)
- "Peaches" (see page 488)
- *Student Writing Handbook* pages 24–25
- Chart paper and a marker
- *Assessment Resource Book*

Note

Alma Flor Ada originally wrote "Lettuce" and "Peaches" in Spanish. Spanish-speaking students might benefit from hearing or reading the poems in Spanish prior to hearing them in English. Both the English and Spanish versions of the poems are reproduced in the *Teacher's Manual* (pages 487–488) and in the *Student Writing Handbook* (pages 24–25).

Signal for the students' attention and have a few volunteers share with the class. Point out that by using words such as *small*, *curly*, *fresh*, *wrinkled*, and *bright green*, the poet helps us imagine the lettuce by describing its size, shape, and color.

2 Read and Discuss "Peaches"

Ask the students to listen as you read another poem by Alma Flor Ada aloud. Read "Peaches" aloud twice, clarifying vocabulary on the first reading.

> **Suggested Vocabulary**
>
> **caress:** touch or hug

Have the students open to *Student Writing Handbook* page 25, where the poem "Peaches" is reproduced. Ask them to follow along as you read the poem again; then ask:

 Q *What words does the poet use to help us imagine the peaches? Turn to your partner.*

Signal for the students' attention and have a few volunteers share with the class. Point out that words such as *juicy*, *golden*, *honey-sweet*, and *caress* help us imagine how the peaches taste, look, and feel.

3 Choose a Food and Generate Descriptive Words

Explain that the students will each write a poem about a favorite food today. Ask:

 Q *What is a favorite food you might write a poem about? Turn to your partner.*

Signal for the students' attention. Have them close their eyes and picture the food in their minds as they listen to the following questions. Ask the questions, pausing between each one to give the students time to think:

Q   *What does your food look like?*

Q   *What does your food taste or smell like?*

Q   *How does it feel in your hand? In your mouth?*

Have the students open their eyes and talk with their partner about what they imagined. After a few moments, signal for their attention and ask:

Q   *What food did you imagine, and what words might you use in a poem about it?*

As volunteers share their thinking, record their ideas on a sheet of chart paper entitled "Food Words."

Food Words

apples	red, round, smooth, crunchy, wet, sweet
spaghetti	long yellow noodles, red tomato sauce, meatballs, yum!
pizza	triangles, crispy crust, mushrooms, chewy, delicious
cherries	red balls with brown stems, small, smooth, juicy
black beans	black, small and round, spicy, hot

Encourage the students to use words like those on the chart to describe how their food looks, feels, and tastes as they write their poems today.

Teacher Note

You may wish to have the students discuss how they might begin their poems by asking, "What words might you use to start your poem?" Possible frames for first lines might be "I love _____" or "_____ is yummy!"

WRITING TIME

4 **Write Food Poems**

Have the students return to their seats and work silently on food poems for 20–30 minutes. Join the students in writing for a few minutes, and then circulate and observe.

> ### CLASS ASSESSMENT NOTE
>
> Observe the students and ask yourself:
>
> - Are the students eager to write?
>
> - Do they use ideas listed on the chart or ideas of their own?
>
> - Are they attempting to write poems rather than stories?
>
> Support students by asking them questions such as:
>
> **Q** *How are you starting your poem?*
>
> **Q** *Close your eyes and imagine your favorite food. What does it [look/feel/taste] like? How can you write that as a line in your poem?*
>
> Record your observations in the *Assessment Resource Book*.

About halfway through the writing time, signal for the students' attention and have them look at their writing as they listen to the following questions. Ask the questions one at a time, pausing between each question to allow time for the students to think.

Q *Are you writing a poem or a story? How do you know?*

Q *If you're writing a story, what can you do to turn it into a poem?*

Have a few volunteers share their thinking with the class, and then have the students resume writing for another 10–15 minutes.

Signal to let the students know when writing time is over.

SHARING AND REFLECTING

5 ▶ Share Poems and Reflect on Getting Ideas

Have a few volunteers read their poems to the class. After each student shares, point out something you liked about the poem, and then invite the class to comment on the poem by asking questions such as:

Q *What did you like about [Sasha's] poem?*

Q *What words did you hear that helped you make pictures in your mind?*

Q *What ideas did you get for your own writing by listening to [Sasha's] poem?*

Explain that next week the students will hear and write more poems.

EXTENSION

Read More Poems by Alma Flor Ada

The poems "Lettuce" and "Peaches" are from *Gathering the Sun: An Alphabet in Spanish and English*, a collection of poems inspired by the lives of migrant farmworkers. Each poem appears in its original Spanish, accompanied by an English translation. If possible, check out a copy of this book from your school or community library and read other poems aloud to the students. Poems with rich language that invites discussion include "César Chávez," "Cherry Stand" ("Kiosco de Cerezas"), and "Rain" ("Lluvia"). You might invite Spanish-speaking students to read the Spanish versions of the poems aloud to their classmates.

Teacher Note

Save the "Food Words" chart to use in Week 2.

Poetry

Tree House
by Shel Silverstein

A tree house, a free house,
A secret you and me house,
A high up in the leafy branches
Cozy as can be house.

A street house, a neat house,
Be sure and wipe your feet house
Is not my kind of house at all—
Let's go live in a tree house.

Poetry

Boa Constrictor
by Shel Silverstein

Oh, I'm being eaten
By a boa constrictor,
A boa constrictor,
A boa constrictor,
I'm being eaten by a boa constrictor.
And I don't like it—one bit.
Well, what do you know?
It's nibblin' my toe.
Oh, gee,
It's up to my knee.
Oh, my,
It's up to my thigh.
Oh, fiddle,
It's up to my middle.
Oh, heck,
It's up to my neck.
Oh, dread,
It's upmmmmmmmmmmmffffffffff...

The Coyote
by Douglas Florian

I prowl.
I growl.
My howl
Is throaty.
I love
A vowel,
For I am coyoᵒᵒᵒote.

The Tiger
by Douglas Florian

I am a cat—come hear me purrrr.
I've many stripes upon my furrrr.
I speed through forests like a blurrrr.
I hunt at night—I am tigerrrr.

Poetry

Knoxville, Tennessee
by Nikki Giovanni

I always like summer
best
you can eat fresh corn
from daddy's garden
and okra
and greens
and cabbage
and lots of
barbecue
and buttermilk
and homemade ice-cream
at the church picnic

and listen to
gospel music
outside
at the church
homecoming
and go to the mountains with
your grandmother
and go barefooted
and be warm
all the time
not only when you go to bed
and sleep

Lettuce

by Alma Flor Ada, English translation by Rosa Zubizarreta

Small, curly,
fresh and wrinkled
heads of bright
green lettuce.

Empty boxes
wait for us
to bend our backs
and fill them up.

....

Lechuga

Cabecitas rizadas
llenas de arrugas
frescas, lozanas,
verdes lechugas.

Cajas y cajas
vacías esperan
que doblen las espaldas
quienes las llenan.

Peaches
by Alma Flor Ada, English translation by Rosa Zubizarreta

Juicy, golden peaches,
honey-sweet,
like a gentle caress
in the palm of my hand.

....

Duraznos

Duraznos jugosos,
almibarados, dorados,
como una caricia suave
en la palma de la mano.

UNIT 6: POEMS AND WORDS

"My Baby Brother"
by Mary Ann Hoberman
(see page 513)

A baby brother is lovingly described in this poem.

"Wind Song"
by Lilian Moore
(see page 514)

In this poem, the wind gives voice to quiet things.

"Weather"
by Aileen Fisher
(see page 515)

This poem lists weather's many sounds.

"Fish"
by Mary Ann Hoberman
(see page 516)

This poem describes all the ways fish move.

Writing Focus

- Students hear, read, and discuss poems.

- Students explore descriptive words in poems.

- Students generate word lists and writing ideas.

- Students write poems using descriptive words.

Social Focus

- Students work in a responsible way.

- Students express interest in and appreciation for one another's writing.

- Students build on one another's thinking.

DO AHEAD

- Prior to Day 2, think of a place in your school where you can take your class to listen to a variety of sounds. Options might include the hallway, the playground, or an area just outside the lunchroom, computer lab, or another classroom. If you are able to hear many sounds from your own classroom, you might stay there for this lesson.

TEACHER AS WRITER

"The poet doesn't invent. He listens."

— *Jean Cocteau*

This week, listen to the sounds of your classroom with a poet's ears. Jot down in your writing notebook things you hear your students saying, as well as any other sounds you hear. Toward the end of the week, read over your notes and shape them into a poem. Keep in mind that the poem does not have to rhyme. Concentrate on using short lines and vivid language.

Day 1

Materials

- "My Baby Brother" (see page 513)
- "Food Words" chart from Week 1
- *Student Writing Handbook* page 26
- Chart paper (both lined and unlined) and a marker
- *Assessment Resource Book*

Exploring Poems

In this lesson, the students:

- Hear, read, and discuss a poem
- Write a shared poem about the classroom clock
- List descriptive words about classroom objects
- Write poems about classroom objects
- Get ideas by listening to one another

GETTING READY TO WRITE

▶1 Read "My Baby Brother" Aloud and Discuss Descriptive Words

Have partners get their notebooks and their *Student Writing Handbooks* and sit together at desks today.

Remind the students that last week they heard two poems by Alma Flor Ada, "Lettuce" and "Peaches," and talked about the words she uses to describe how lettuce and peaches look, feel, and taste. Direct their attention to the "Food Woods" chart and review that they brainstormed a list of descriptive words about favorite foods and used some of the words to write their own food poems. Explain that this week they will hear more poems with descriptive words and use descriptive words in poems they write.

Tell the students that today they will hear the poem "My Baby Brother" by Mary Ann Hoberman. Invite the students to listen for descriptive words as you read.

Read the poem aloud twice, slowly and clearly, clarifying vocabulary on the first reading.

Making Meaning® Teacher

Your students will be familiar with "My Baby Brother" since it is used in *Making Meaning* Unit 3, Week 1. Remind them that they have heard the poem, and explain that today they will hear it again and think about it from the point of view of a writer.

Suggested Vocabulary

velvet: smooth and soft

dimple: small hollow in a person's cheek or chin

Have the students open to *Student Writing Handbook* page 26, where "My Baby Brother" is reproduced. Ask them to follow along as you read the poem again; then ask:

 Q *What words does the poet use to describe how her baby brother looks? Turn to your partner.*

Signal for the students' attention and have a few volunteers share with the class. Point out that the poet uses descriptive words like *tiny*, *soft*, *velvet brown*, and *curled up tight* to help us picture the baby in our minds.

2 ▶ Write a Shared Poem About the Classroom Clock

Explain that the students will use descriptive words to write poems about objects in the classroom today. Ask:

Q *What objects in the classroom could we write poems about?*

Have a few volunteers share their ideas. Explain that the class will write a poem together to model what they will do on their own during writing time.

Ask the students to look carefully at the classroom clock as they listen to the following questions. Ask the questions one at a time, pausing between each to give the students time to think.

Q *What words describe the clock's shape?*

Q *What words describe its color? Its size?*

Q *What other words describe the clock?*

Repeat each question and have a few volunteers share their thinking with the class. Record their ideas on a sheet of chart paper entitled "Words That Describe the Clock."

Words That Describe the Clock

round like a circle

black all around

white in the middle

black numbers in a circle, 1 to 12

hands point to the numbers

one short hand and one long hand

At the top of a sheet of lined chart paper, write the words "Classroom Clock" and explain that this is the title of the poem. Explain that you will begin the poem similarly to "My Baby Brother," with the words "The classroom clock is beautiful." Write this line on the chart, and then ask:

Q *What could we write as the second line of the poem?*

Encourage the students to look at the "Words That Describe the Clock" chart for ideas. Use the students' suggestions to write three more lines to complete a first stanza, and then use their suggestions to write a second stanza.

Teacher Note ▶

If the students have difficulty suggesting lines for the poem, model writing a line or two yourself using words on the "Words That Describe the Clock" chart.

Classroom Clock

The classroom clock is beautiful,

So round like a circle.

It has a white face

And a black rim all around.

Its one short hand and one long hand

Point to crisp black numbers.

From 1 to 12 they march around

Tick, tick, tick!

As a class, read the poem aloud.

3 ▶ Choose Objects and Write Descriptive Words

Explain that today the students will each pick an object in the classroom, list words that describe the object, and write a poem about it. Give the students a moment to look around the room and silently choose an object.

Explain that the students will look at the object as they listen to questions about it and then write words that come to mind about the object. Have them open their notebooks to the next blank page, and then ask the following questions, pausing between each question to give the students time to write a few words.

Q *What does the object look like? List some words that come to mind.*

Q *What words describe its shape? List them.*

Q *What words describe its color? List them.*

Q *What words describe its size? List them.*

Have partners read their list of words to each other without telling each other what their objects are, and then have them try to guess each other's objects from the descriptions.

After a few minutes, signal for the students' attention, and ask:

Q *What words helped you guess the object?*

Explain that the students will write poems about what their objects look like using some of the words they listed. Tell them that they may begin their poem with the line "_____ is beautiful" or with any other words they choose.

WRITING TIME

4 ▶ Write Poems About Classroom Objects

Have the students work silently on poems about classroom objects for 20–30 minutes. Join them in writing for a few minutes, and then circulate and observe.

CLASS ASSESSMENT NOTE

Observe the students and ask yourself:

* Are the students eager to write?

* Do they use their listed descriptive words or other words of their own?

* Are they attempting to write poems rather than stories?

Support struggling students by having them look at their objects as you repeat the questions in Step 3. Encourage them to add to their poems by asking, "What other words tell what [your lunch box] looks like? Where might you add those words to your poem?"

Record your observations in the *Assessment Resource Book*.

Signal to let the students know when writing time is over.

SHARING AND REFLECTING

5 ▶ Share Lines from Poems and Reflect on Getting Ideas

Have the students review their poems and each underline one line to share with the class. Encourage them to choose a line that they really like and that has words that describe how their object looks. After allowing a moment for them to choose their lines, go around the room and, without comment, have each student read her chosen line aloud.

After all of the students have shared, ask and briefly discuss:

Q *What did you hear that got you interested in someone else's poem?*

Q *[Deirdre], read your line again. What object do you think [Deirdre's] line might describe?*

Q *What ideas did you get for your own writing by listening to [Deirdre's] line?*

Explain that tomorrow the students will hear and write poems with words that describe sounds.

Day 2

Materials

- "Wind Song" (see page 514)
- *Student Writing Handbook* page 27
- Chart paper (both lined and unlined) and a marker
- Location in the school to listen to sounds (see "Do Ahead" on page 491)

Exploring Poems

In this lesson, the students:

- Hear, read, and discuss a poem
- Move around the school responsibly
- Listen to sounds in the school
- Write a shared poem about school sounds

GETTING READY TO WRITE

 Read "Wind Song" Aloud

Have the students begin the lesson at their desks. Remind them that yesterday they heard the poem "My Baby Brother" and each wrote a poem that describes how something *looks*. Explain that today they will hear two poems with words that describe how things *sound*.

Ask the students to close their eyes and listen as you read "Wind Song" by Lilian Moore aloud twice. Clarify vocabulary on the first reading.

> **Suggested Vocabulary**
>
> **ashcans:** garbage cans

Have the students open to *Student Writing Handbook* page 27, where "Wind Song" is reproduced. Have them follow along as you read the poem aloud again; then ask:

Q *What sound words do you notice in this poem?*

As the students share, record the words on a sheet of chart paper labeled "Sound Words."

```
Sound Words

sigh

swish

snap

whistle

hum

speak

whisper
```

Point out that by including many sound words, the poet helps us hear and imagine what happens when the wind blows.

Explain that you will take the students to a place in the school where they can listen to sounds. When they return to the class, they will write a shared poem about that place. Point out that, like Lilian Moore, they will try to include many sound words in the poem to describe what the place is like. Tell the students where you will take them, and then ask:

Q *What kinds of sounds might we hear [in the hallway]?*

▶ **Discuss Moving Responsibly Around the School**

State how you expect the students to move from the classroom to the location where they will listen for sounds; then ask and briefly discuss:

Q *What do we need to do to make sure we don't disturb others in the school?*

Q *How else will you work responsibly during this activity?*

Teacher Note

You might say, "This will be a silent activity. When I point to your table, you will each get your notebook and pencil and line up. Then, you will follow me [to the hallway] where I will point to show you where to sit. Once you are seated, start listening for sounds and write words that describe them in your notebook. When I give the signal to return, quietly stand up and move back into the classroom."

FACILITATION TIP

Continue to **avoid repeating or paraphrasing** students' responses. Help them learn to participate responsibly in class discussions by encouraging them to ask one another to speak up or to ask a question if they don't understand what a classmate has said. (See the front matter in volume 1 for special considerations for English Language Learners.)

Students might say:

"We need to make sure that we walk very quietly."

"In addition to what [Ramon] said, if we see someone we know, we shouldn't shout to them. Maybe we could just wave."

"I'll start listening and writing as soon as I sit down."

"I won't bother the person sitting next to me."

Tell the students that you will check in with them after the activity to see how they did.

Teacher Note ▶

If the students do not meet your expectations as they move from the classroom to the location, stop and have them return to the classroom. Restate your expectations, and then try again. If this takes longer than a single class period to accomplish, continue the lesson tomorrow.

3▶ Listen for and List School Sounds

Take the students to the location you selected and have them listen for and list sounds they hear.

After about 5 minutes, have the students follow you back to the classroom and return to their seats. Ask and briefly discuss:

Q *What did you do to move and act responsibly during this activity?*

Q *What problems did we have? Why do we want to avoid those problems in the future? What can we do differently next time?*

4▶ Add to the "Sound Words" Chart

Ask the students to open their notebooks to their list of school sounds. Ask:

Q *What sounds did you hear [in the hallway]?*

As the students share, add their words to the "Sound Words" chart. If the students describe things that made sounds (such as a chair scraping the floor), list these and follow up by asking:

Q *What sound did [the chair scraping the floor] make?*

Sound Words

sigh

swish

snap

whistle

hum

speak

whisper

chair scraping the floor—screech

door slamming shut—bang!

laughing

talking

basketball bouncing—thump thump thump

Mr. Makebe's whistle—tweet tweet

WRITING TIME

5 ▶ **Write a Shared Poem About School Sounds**

Label a sheet of lined chart paper "School Sounds" and explain that the poem you will write today will begin and end similarly to "Wind Song." On the chart, write the words *When it is daytime at our school/ The quiet things speak.* Then ask:

Q   *What could we write as the next line of the poem?*

Encourage the students to look at the "Sound Words" chart to get ideas, and use the students' suggestions to write a poem. It is not necessary to continue to follow the structure of "Wind Song."

◀ **Teacher Note**

If the students have difficulty suggesting lines for the poem, stimulate their thinking by writing one or two lines yourself using words from the "Sound Words" chart.

> ### School Sounds
>
> When it is daytime at our school
> The quiet things speak.
> Chairs scrape. Doors bang.
> Children talk and laugh.
> Thump thump thump
> A basketball bounces.
> Mr. Makebe blows his whistle
> Tweet tweet tweeeeeet!
>
> When it is night
> suddenly
> then,
> the quiet things
> are quiet again.

SHARING AND REFLECTING

▶ 6 Reflect on Writing the Shared Poem

As a class, read the poem aloud. Ask and briefly discuss:

Q *What do you think a reader might imagine about our school when he or she reads this poem?*

Explain that tomorrow the students will write their own poems using sound words. Encourage them to listen for interesting sounds between now and then and to write them in their notebooks, if they can.

Teacher Note

Save the "Sound Words" chart and the "School Sounds" poem to use on Day 3 and throughout the unit.

Day 3

Exploring Poems

In this lesson, the students:

* Hear, read, and discuss a poem
* Generate and list sound words
* Write poems using sound words
* Get ideas by listening to one another
* Ask one another questions about their writing

GETTING READY TO WRITE

▶ 1 Review and Add to the "Sound Words" Chart

Have partners get their notebooks and *Student Writing Handbooks* and sit together at desks today. Remind the students that yesterday they contributed to a shared poem entitled "School Sounds." Read the poem aloud together, and point out that they included sounds to help readers imagine their school.

Review the "Sound Words" chart and ask:

Q *What other sounds have you heard that we can add to the chart?*

Add any suggestions to the chart. Explain that you will read another sound poem, and then the students will write their own poems using sound words.

▶ 2 Read and Discuss "Weather"

Tell the students that they will hear the poem "Weather" by Aileen Fisher. Invite them to listen for sounds and to think about the type of weather the poem describes. Read the poem aloud twice, and then have the students open to *Student Writing Handbook* page 28,

Materials

* "Weather" (see page 515)
* Charted "School Sounds" poem from Day 2
* "Sound Words" chart from Day 2
* *Student Writing Handbook* page 28

where "Weather" is reproduced. Have the students follow along as you read the poem aloud again; then ask:

Q *What kind of weather do you imagine when you read this poem? What words make you imagine that?*

Q *Do you think this is a quiet poem or a loud poem? Why?*

> **Students might say:**
>
> "I imagine wind from the words 'rustles' and 'whishes.'"
>
> "The word 'splishes' makes me think it's raining."
>
> "This is a loud poem! It has lots of sound words in it."
>
> "I disagree with [Misha]. I think it starts out kind of quiet with words like 'sings and rustles and pings' and ends loudly with 'CRASHES.'"

Ask:

Q *What sound words in this poem can we add to our "Sound Words" chart?*

Add the students' suggestions to the "Sound Words" chart.

▶ **3 Prepare to Write Poems Using Sound Words**

Ask:

Q *What things make lots of sounds that you might write a poem about?*

> **Students might say:**
>
> "I could write a poem about playing soccer. There are lots of sounds on the soccer field."
>
> "The park has a lot of sounds."
>
> "I could write a poem about my alarm clock waking me up in the morning."
>
> "I could write about going to the flea market with my mom."

Explain that the students may begin their poems the same way "Weather" begins, with the line "_____ is full of the nicest sounds," or they may begin the poems any way they choose. Encourage them to use words from the "Sound Words" chart and any other sound words they can think of in their poems.

WRITING TIME

4 ▶ Write Poems Using Sound Words

Have the students work silently on poems with sound words for 20–30 minutes. Join them in writing for a few minutes, and then begin conferring with individual students.

TEACHER CONFERENCE NOTE

During the coming week, confer with individual students about their poems. Have each student read his poem aloud, and ask yourself:

* Does the student's writing communicate clearly? If not, what's unclear?

* Is the student attempting to write a poem, rather than a story?

* Has the student used descriptive words to show how things look or sound?

Support students during the conference by using one or more of the following techniques:

* Have the student close his eyes and listen as you read the poem back to him. Ask him what else he imagined and what other words he could include in the poem.

* Review the charted descriptive words and ask the student to choose some to use in his poem.

* If a student has difficulty starting a poem, begin one together by adapting the first line or lines of one of the poems reproduced in the *Student Writing Handbook*. Have him continue the poem.

Document your observations for each student using the "Conference Notes" record sheet (BLM1). Use the "Conference Notes" record sheets during conferences throughout this unit.

Signal to let the students know when writing time is over.

SHARING AND REFLECTING

 Share Lines from Poems and Reflect

Have the students review their poems and each underline one line to share with the class. Encourage them to choose a line in which they describe the sound of something. After allowing a moment for them to choose their lines, go around the room and, without comment, have each student read his line aloud.

When all of the students have finished sharing, ask and briefly discuss:

Q *What sound words did you hear that got you interested in someone else's writing?*

Q *[Anthony], read us your line again. What do you want to ask [Anthony] about [his] line?*

Q *What ideas did you get for your own writing by listening to [Anthony's] line?*

Explain that tomorrow the students will hear and write poems with words that describe how something moves.

Day 4

Exploring Poems

In this lesson, the students:

- Hear, read, and discuss a poem
- Discuss movement words in a poem
- Generate and list movement words
- Write shared and individual poems using movement words
- Ask one another questions about their writing
- Get ideas by listening to one another

GETTING READY TO WRITE

1 ▶ Read "Fish" Aloud and Discuss Movement Words

Have partners get their notebooks and *Student Writing Handbooks* and sit together at desks today. Direct their attention to the charts of words from the past two weeks and remind them that they have been exploring words that describe how things look and sound. Explain that today they will explore words that describe how things move.

Tell the students that you will read the poem "Fish" by Mary Ann Hoberman, and remind them that they heard the poem "My Baby Brother" by the same author earlier in the week. Invite the students to listen for words that describe how fish move.

Read the poem aloud twice, slowly and clearly, clarifying vocabulary on the first reading.

Suggested Vocabulary

flit: move quickly back and forth
lickety-split: very fast
bound: jump

Materials

- "Fish" (see page 516)
- Charts of words from Weeks 1 and 2
- *Student Writing Handbook* page 29
- Chart paper (both lined and unlined) and a marker

 ELL Note

You may want to have the students act out the poem as you read it aloud. Dramatizing can help English Language Learners understand the words in the poem.

Have the students open to *Student Writing Handbook* page 29, where "Fish" is reproduced. Have the students follow along as you read the poem aloud again; then ask:

Q   *What do you notice about how the poet wrote this poem?*

 Q   *What words in the poem tell how fish move? Turn to your partner.*

Signal for the students' attention and have several volunteers share their thinking with the class. Record the words they report on a sheet of chart paper entitled "Movement Words."

Movement Words

Flit

wiggling

swiggling

swerving

scurrying

whizzing

Flying

leap

bound

2 Write a Shared Poem About Something That Moves

Explain that the class will write a shared poem, similar to "Fish," about something that moves. Use "Think, Pair, Share" to have partners first think about and then discuss:

 Q   *What are some things that move that we might write a poem about?* [pause] *Turn to your partner.*

Signal for the students' attention and have a few volunteers share with the class. Record their ideas on a sheet of chart paper entitled "Things That Move."

◄ Teacher Note

If the students have difficulty generating ideas, stimulate their thinking by suggesting some ideas from the diagram.

```
┌─────────────────────────────────────────────┐
│                                               │
│            Things That Move                   │
│                                               │
│      horses                                   │
│                                               │
│      trucks                                    │
│                                               │
│      bikes                                     │
│                                               │
│      skateboards                               │
│                                               │
│      airplanes                                 │
│                                               │
│      kids                                      │
│                                               │
│      our guinea pig                            │
│                                               │
│      Ferris wheels                             │
│                                               │
└─────────────────────────────────────────────┘
```

Choose one of the ideas on the "Things That Move" chart and write it at the top of a sheet of lined chart paper. Underneath this, write a first line for a poem that is similar to the first line of "Fish" (for example, *Look at horses run*). Then ask:

Q *What words might we write under this line to describe how [horses run]?*

Encourage the students to look at the "Movement Words" chart to get ideas, and add new words to the chart as students suggest them. Use the students' suggestions to write a poem that is similar in structure to the poem "Fish."

Horses

Look at horses run.

Galloping

Hoofing

Pounding

Breathing

Turning

Dusting

Sweating

All of them making a big

BIG

BIG

BIG

Sound.

Invite the students to make a picture in their minds as they read the poem aloud together.

WRITING TIME

 Write Poems About Things That Move

Explain that today the students will each choose something that moves and write a poem about it. They may pick something on the "Things That Move" chart or they may choose anything else. Tell them that they may write a poem that is similar to "Fish" or one that is different. Encourage them to include movement words to help their readers make pictures in their minds.

Have the students work silently on poems with movement words for 20–30 minutes. Join them in writing for a few minutes, and then confer with individual students.

TEACHER CONFERENCE NOTE

Continue to confer with individual students. Have each student read her poem aloud, and ask yourself:

- Does the student's writing communicate clearly? If not, what's unclear?

- Is the student attempting to write a poem, rather than a story?

- Has the student used descriptive words to show how things look, sound, or move?

Support students during the conference by using one or more of the following techniques:

- Have the student close her eyes and listen as you read the poem back to her. Ask her what else she imagined and what other words she could include in the poem.

- Review the charted descriptive words and ask the student to choose some to use in her poem.

- If a student has difficulty starting a poem, begin one together by adapting the first line or lines of one of the poems reproduced in the *Student Writing Handbook*. Have her continue the poem.

Document your observations for each student using the "Conference Notes" record sheet (BLM1).

Signal to let the students know when writing time is over.

SHARING AND REFLECTING

 ### Share Lines from Poems and Reflect

Have the students review their poems and each underline one line to share with the class. Encourage them to choose a line in which they describe how something moves. After allowing a moment for them to choose their lines, go around the room and, without comment, have each student read her line aloud.

When all of the students have finished sharing, ask and briefly discuss:

Q *What did you hear that got you interested in someone else's writing?*

Q *[Asha], read us your line again. What do you want to ask [Asha] about [her] line?*

Q *What ideas did you get for your own writing by listening to [Asha's] line?*

Explain that the students will continue to write poems next week, and they will choose one to publish in a class book and share from the Author's Chair.

EXTENSION

Listen to Poems and Draw Visualizations

Help the students continue to explore descriptive language by showing and reading aloud one of the poems you have previously read aloud to the students. Have the students close their eyes and make a mental picture of the poem as you read it. Then have them draw their visualizations. Invite the students to share their pictures with the class. Have them point out the words in the poem that helped them draw their picture.

Teacher Note

Save the "Movement Words" chart to use during Week 3.

My Baby Brother

by Mary Ann Hoberman

My baby brother's beautiful,
So perfect and so tiny.
His skin is soft and velvet brown;
His eyes are dark and shiny.

His hair is black and curled up tight;
His two new teeth are sharp and white.
I like it when he chews his toes;
And when he laughs, his dimple shows.

Wind Song

by Lilian Moore

When the wind blows
the quiet things speak.
Some whisper, some clang,
Some creak.

Grasses swish.
Treetops sigh.
Flags slap
and snap at the sky.
Wires on poles
whistle and hum.
Ashcans roll.
Windows drum.

When the wind goes—
suddenly
then,
the quiet things
are quiet again.

Weather

by Aileen Fisher

Weather is full
of the nicest sounds:
it sings
and rustles
and pings
and pounds
and hums
and tinkles
and strums
and twangs
and whishes
and sprinkles
and splishes
and bangs
and mumbles
and grumbles
and rumbles
and flashes
and CRASHES.

Poetry

Fish

by Mary Ann Hoberman

Look at them flit
Lickety-split
Wiggling
Swiggling
Swerving
Curving
Hurrying
Scurrying
Chasing
Racing
Whizzing
Whisking
Flying
Frisking
Tearing around
With a leap and a bound
But none of them making the tiniest
                    tiniest
                tiniest
            tiniest
        sound.

Week 3 Overview

UNIT 6: POEMS AND WORDS

"Clouds"
by Christina G. Rossetti
(see page 537)

This poem describes clouds as white sheep on a blue hill.

"Rain Poem"
by Elizabeth Coatsworth
(see page 538)

This poem says rain is like a small, gray mouse.

"The Steam Shovel"
by Rowena Bennett
(see page 539)

A steam shovel is compared to a dinosaur in this poem.

Writing Focus

- Students hear, read, and discuss poems.

- Students explore figurative language in poems.

- Students informally use figurative language to write poems.

- Students each choose one poem to publish in a class book.

- Students present their poems from the Author's Chair.

Social Focus

- Students express interest in and appreciation for one another's writing.

- Students listen respectfully to the thinking of others and share their own.

DO AHEAD

- Prior to Day 1, copy the poems "Clouds" and "Rain Poem" (pages 537 and 538) onto chart paper.

- (Optional) If computers are available, consider recruiting parent volunteers to help the students type their poems on Day 3.

TEACHER AS WRITER

"Everything I see or hear can become a poem."
— *Jack Prelutsky*

Select a classroom object or an object at home, such as a TV, refrigerator, or floor lamp. Study it. Think about its size, shape, features, and function. Then think of a person, animal, or thing the object reminds you of. Write a poem about the object. You might begin your poem with the line *A _____ is a _____* (for example, *A coffeepot is a trusted friend*).

Day 1

Materials

- "Clouds" (see page 537)
- "Rain Poem" (see page 538)
- Chart of "Clouds" (see "Do Ahead" on page 519)
- Chart of "Rain Poem" (see "Do Ahead" on page 519)
- Chart paper (both lined and unlined) and a marker

FACILITATION TIP

Reflect on your experience over the past three weeks with **avoiding repeating or paraphrasing** students' responses. Does this practice feel natural to you? Are you integrating it into class discussions throughout the school day? What effect is it having on the students? Are they participating more responsibly in class discussions? Continue to try this practice and reflect on students' responses as you facilitate class discussions in the future. (See the front matter in volume 1 for special considerations for English Language Learners.)

Exploring Poems

In this lesson, the students:

- Hear, read, and discuss poems
- Explore figurative language
- Write shared and individual poems about rain
- Express interest in and appreciation for one another's writing
- Share their partner's writing with the class

About Figurative Language in Grade 2

During Days 1 and 2 of this week, the students explore poems with metaphors and similes, and informally use figurative language to write poems about classroom objects. This brief introduction to figurative language lays the foundation for further study in later grades. The students are not expected to identify or name metaphors or similes at this stage.

GETTING READY TO WRITE

▶1 Read and Discuss "Clouds"

Gather the class with partners sitting together, facing you. Have the students bring their notebooks with them. Review that the students have been exploring and writing poems using descriptive words to help their readers imagine how things look, sound, and move in their poems. Explain that today they will hear two poems that use descriptive words in a different way.

Ask the students to close their eyes and listen as you read "Clouds" by Christina G. Rossetti aloud; then direct their attention to the charted "Clouds" poem and invite them to read it along with you. Read the poem aloud together; then ask and briefly discuss:

Q *Is this poem about clouds or sheep, and why do you think so?*

Students might say:

"The title says it's about clouds, but it only talks about sheep, so
  it's about sheep."

"I disagree with [Jin] because wind doesn't make sheep stop or go.
  It's about clouds."

"I agree with [Polly]. It's about clouds. The clouds are like white sheep."

If necessary, point out that the poet writes about clouds as if they
are sheep.

2 ▶ Read "Rain Poem" Aloud

Tell the students that you will read another poem in which the poet
talks about one thing as if it is something else. Ask the students
to close their eyes and listen as you read "Rain Poem" by Elizabeth
Coatsworth aloud; then direct their attention to the charted poem
and invite them to read it along with you. Read "Rain Poem" aloud
together; then ask and briefly discuss:

Q *Is this poem about rain or mice, and why do you think so?*

Students might say:

"In this poem it says rain is *like* a mouse. So it's about rain."

"I agree with [Alberto]. The poem tells how rain is the same as a
  mouse. It is quiet and gray."

"I also agree. Another way they are alike is that sometimes rain
  gets inside the house, and a mouse does, too."

Point out that poets often write about one thing as if it is like another.

3 ▶ Write a Shared Poem About Rain

Direct the students' attention to the first line of "Rain Poem" and point
out that this poet imagines that rain is like a mouse. Use "Think, Pair,
Share" to have partners first think about and then discuss:

Q *If we were going to write our own "Rain Poem," what other things
    might we say that rain is like?* [pause] *Turn to your partner.*

◀ **Teacher Note**

Poets often use metaphors
and similes in their poems. A
metaphor is a type of figurative
language in which a poet
describes something by calling it
something else, for example, "A
train is a dragon." A comparison of
two things using the words "like"
or "as" is a *simile*, for example, "The
rain was like a little mouse." The
students do not need to know
or use these terms at this point.

Grade Two | 521

Teacher Note ▶

If the students have difficulty generating ideas, suggest a few from the diagram to stimulate their thinking.

Signal for the students' attention and have a few volunteers share their ideas with the class. Record their ideas on a sheet of chart paper entitled "The rain is like _____."

The rain is like _____.

a curtain

candy drops

a snake

music

glitter

falling stars

At the top of a sheet of lined chart paper, write the title "Another Rain Poem." Select one of the ideas from the chart "The rain is like _____" and use it to write a first line for a poem below the title.

Teacher Note ▶

If the students have difficulty suggesting lines for the poem, model writing one or two more lines yourself.

Use the students' suggestions to write a few more lines for the poem. (It is not necessary to follow the structure of "Rain Poem.") Elicit the students' ideas by asking questions such as:

Q *How is rain is like [a curtain]?*

Q *What words describe how rain looks?*

Q *What words describe how rain sounds?*

Q *What words describe how rain moves?*

> ### Another Rain Poem
>
> The rain is like a curtain
>
> That comes down from the sky.
>
> When the curtain falls
>
> Plop plop plop
>
> Everything stops.
>
> We run inside and wait.
>
> Soon the curtain opens
>
> And the sun begins to shine.
>
> Then we run outside again.

Reread the poem together as a class. Explain that the students will write their own rain poem today, beginning with the line "The rain is like _____." They may choose an idea from the chart "The rain is like _____" or they may use an idea of their own. Encourage the students to include words that describe how the rain looks, sounds, and moves.

WRITING TIME

 4 Write Poems About Rain

Have partners move to sit together at desks and work silently on poems about rain for 20–30 minutes. Join them in writing for a few minutes, and then confer with individual students.

TEACHER CONFERENCE NOTE

As you did last week, continue to confer with individual students. Have each student read his poem aloud, and ask yourself:

● Does the student's writing communicate clearly? If not, what's unclear?

● Is the student attempting to write a poem, rather than a story?

● Has the student used descriptive words to show how things look, sound, or move?

Support students during the conference by using one or more of the following techniques:

● Have the student close his eyes and listen as you read the poem back to him. Ask him what else he imagined and what other words he could include in the poem.

● Review the charted descriptive words and ask the student to choose some to use in his poem.

● If a student has difficulty starting a poem, begin one together by adapting the first line or lines of one of the poems reproduced in the *Student Writing Handbook*. Have him continue the poem.

Document your observations for each student using the "Conference Notes" record sheet (BLM1).

Signal to let the students know when writing time is over.

SHARING AND REFLECTING

 Share Poems in Pairs

Explain that partners will read their poems to each other. Encourage them to tell each other the words they find interesting or something they like about the other's poem. Alert them to listen carefully, as they will share information about their partner's poem with the class. Have partners share their poems with each other.

After a few minutes, signal for the students' attention and ask:

Q *What does your partner think rain is like?*

Q *What are some descriptive words your partner used that helped you imagine the rain?*

Explain that tomorrow the students will hear another poem where the poet writes about something as though it were something else.

Teacher Note

Save the charts of the poems "Clouds" and "Rain Poem" to use on Day 2. Also, save the chart "The rain is like _____" to use on Day 2.

Day 2

Materials

- "The Steam Shovel" (see page 539)
- *Student Writing Handbook* page 30
- "The rain is like _____" chart from Day 1
- Charts of "Clouds" and "Rain Poem" from Day 1
- Charts of words from Weeks 1 and 2

Teacher Note

If possible, show a picture of a steam shovel (or similar machine) or facilitate a discussion about steam shovels by asking, "Have you ever seen a steam shovel or something like it? Tell us about it." (You may want to mention that a steam shovel is operated using steam power, as train engines used to be, but that steam-powered shovels are rare today; most construction equipment is now powered by gasoline or diesel fuel.)

 ELL Note

You might have the students act out the poem as you read it aloud. Dramatizing can help English Language Learners understand the words in a poem.

Exploring Poems

In this lesson, the students:

- Hear, read, and discuss a poem
- Explore figurative language in a poem
- Write poems about anything they choose
- Express interest in and appreciation for one another's writing
- Share their partner's writing with the class

GETTING READY TO WRITE

▶1 Read "The Steam Shovel" Aloud

Gather the class with partners sitting together, facing you. Have them bring their notebooks and their *Student Writing Handbooks* with them. Remind the students that yesterday they heard the poems "Clouds" and "Rain Poem" and thought about how poets sometimes talk about one thing as if it is another. Explain that today they will hear another poem like this.

Tell the students that the poem they will hear is entitled "The Steam Shovel," and is by Rowena Bennett. Explain that a steam shovel is a large machine that is used to dig up loads of dirt in one place and dump them in another.

Ask the students to close their eyes and listen as you read "The Steam Shovel" aloud twice, clarifying vocabulary on the first reading.

> **Suggested Vocabulary**
>
> **crouches:** bends low to the ground

ELL Vocabulary

English Language Learners may benefit from discussing additional vocabulary, including:

beast: animal

paws: feet

jaws: mouth

stiff: straight

Ask and briefly discuss:

Q *What did you imagine as you listened to the poem?*

Students might say:

"I imagined a huge dinosaur taking big bites of dirt."

"I imagined the steam shovel spitting out the dirt."

"I saw it swinging its neck around to dump the dirt."

Point out that the poet writes about a steam shovel as if it were a dinosaur. Have the students open to *Student Writing Handbook* page 30, where "The Steam Shovel" is reproduced. Have the students follow along as you read the poem aloud again; then ask:

Q *What words in the poem tell us that the steam shovel is like a dinosaur?*

Students might say:

"It says, 'He snorts and roars.' That's like a dinosaur."

"It also says, 'He crouches low on his tractor paws.'"

"It says that the steam shovel 'swings his long stiff neck around.' Dinosaurs have long necks, too."

Explain that today the students may write poems about any topic they choose. If they wish, they might try writing a poem like "Steam Shovel," "Rain Poem," or "Clouds," in which they write about something as if it is something else. Briefly review the chart "The rain is like _____" and the other charts of words from earlier in the unit and remind the students to look at the charts to get ideas for descriptive words to include in their poems.

◀ **Teacher Note**

Keep in mind that in this unit the students are exposed to figurative language in a very informal way. They are not expected to use it in their own independent writing, although some students may be able to do so.

WRITING TIME

Write Poems

Have partners move to sit together at desks and work silently on poems for 20–30 minutes. Join them in writing for a few minutes, and then confer with individual students.

TEACHER CONFERENCE NOTE

Continue to confer with individual students. Have each student read her poem aloud to you, and ask yourself:

* Does the student's writing communicate clearly? If not, what's unclear?

* Is the student attempting to write a poem, rather than a story?

* Has the student used descriptive words to show how things look, sound, or move?

Support students during the conference by using one or more of the following techniques:

* Have the student close her eyes and listen as you read the poem back to her. Ask her what else she imagined and what other words she could include in the poem.

* Review the charted descriptive words and ask the student to choose some to use in her poem.

Document your observations for each student using the "Conference Notes" record sheet (BLM1).

Signal to let the students know when writing time is over.

SHARING AND REFLECTING

Share Poems in Pairs

Explain that partners will read their poems to each other, as they did yesterday. Encourage them to tell each other the words they find interesting or something they like in the other's poem. Alert them to listen carefully, as they will share information about their partner's poem with the class. Have partners share their poems with each other.

After a few minutes, signal for the students' attention and ask:

Q   *Did your partner write about something as if it is something else? Tell us about it. [Tinesha], read us your poem.*

Q   *What are some words your partner used that really helped you make pictures in your mind?*

Explain that tomorrow the students will each select one of their poems to share with the class and to publish in a book for the classroom library.

EXTENSION

Read More Poems with Figurative Language

Continue to have the students explore poems with figurative language. Select poems from your classroom or school library. For each poem, have the students close their eyes and make a picture in their minds as you read the poem aloud twice. Then conduct one of the following activities:

● Have the students suggest other things they might compare the subject of the poem to, and then have the class write a poem together using one of them.

● Have the students make a drawing of what they saw in their minds and write their own poem about the drawing underneath it.

● Have partners tell each other what they pictured. Have them write a poem together about a topic similar to that of the poem they heard.

Day 3

Materials

- Charts of words from Weeks 1–3
- *Student Writing Handbooks*
- Loose, lined paper for final versions
- (Optional) Computers for word processing (see "Do Ahead" on page 519)

Proofreading and Writing Final Versions

In this lesson, the students:

- Select poems to publish in a class book
- Revise their poems
- Proofread their poems for spelling
- Write final versions of poems

About Publishing Students' Poems

Today the students each choose a poem to include in a class book of poems. You may decide to publish the students' poetry in some other way. For example, you might display the poems on a classroom or school bulletin board or at the school or community library. Alternatively, you might invite another class or your students' parents to hear the students read their poems during a poetry party. Students can also publish their poems at various websites. To find appropriate websites, search using the keywords "publishing student poetry."

GETTING READY TO WRITE

1 ▶ Discuss Writing Poems

Have partners bring their notebooks and *Student Writing Handbooks* and sit together at desks today. Review that during the last few weeks the students heard and talked about many poems and wrote several poems of their own. Ask and briefly discuss:

Q *What have you learned about poems?*

> **Students might say:**
>
> "Poems look different from stories and are shorter."
>
> "In addition to what [Pedro] said, I think poems have words that help you imagine."
>
> "Poems can be about different things, like food or a tree."
>
> "In addition to what [Bette] said, poems sometimes talk about something as if it were something else."

2 ▶ Review Poems and Choose One for the Class Book

Tell the students that today they will reread the poems they have
written during the past few weeks and choose one they like the best
to publish for the class. Explain that you will collect their poems in a
book to keep in the classroom library for them and others to enjoy.
Ask and briefly discuss:

Q *As you read your poems, what might you look for to help you
decide which poem you like the best?*

Students might say:

"I might look for the one I think is the funniest."

"I can look for one that has good descriptive words."

"I'll look for one where I used my imagination."

Have the students quietly reread their poems and choose one for
the class book. After a few minutes, signal for their attention and
have partners tell each other the poem they chose. Have partners
ask each other why they chose that poem.

3 ▶ Think About Adding to or Changing Poems

Explain that the students will quietly reread their poems and think
about any words they might want to add or change to make the
poems more interesting or fun to read. Direct their attention to the
charted words from Weeks 1–3 and encourage them to look at the
charts for ideas.

Give the students a few minutes to make additions or changes to
their poems.

4 ▶ Proofread Poems for Spelling

Tell the students that today they will copy their chosen poems in
their best handwriting for the class book. Since their poems will be
in a book for others to read, they need to be as free of spelling errors
as possible. Ask them to reread their poems and circle any words
they are unsure how to spell. When most students are finished, ask:

Q *What words have you circled so far?*

◀ **Teacher Note**

If the students have difficulty
answering the question, offer
some ideas like those in the
"Student might say" note and ask,
"What else might you look for?"

◀ **Teacher Note**

If necessary, explain that if the
students want to add words,
they can write them in where
they want them to go. If they
want to change a word, they
can cross out the old word and
write the new word above it.

Have one or two volunteers say the words they circled. Remind the students that the first place they should go to check the spelling of a word is the word bank in their *Student Writing Handbook*. Ask:

Teacher Note ▶

The students might check the spelling of a word by asking another student, asking you, finding the word in a published book, or looking it up in a dictionary or online.

Q   *If the word does not appear in the word bank, what will you do to check the correct spelling?*

Review that each page of the word bank has blank lines where the students can add new words they have learned how to spell correctly.

Explain that during writing time today the students will check and correct their spelling, and then copy their poems for publication.

WRITING TIME

Teacher Note

If you want the students to illustrate their poems, you might provide paper with space for an illustration. ▶

5 ▶ **Write Final Versions**

Have the students check and correct their spelling. As the students finish correcting their spelling, distribute lined writing paper and have the students copy their poems onto it. As the students work, confer with individual students.

TEACHER CONFERENCE NOTE

Confer with individual students about their selected poems. Have each student read his chosen poem aloud, and ask yourself:

- Does the student's writing communicate clearly? If not, what's unclear?

- Did the student write a poem, rather than a story?

- Has the student used descriptive words to show how things look, sound, or move?

- Did the student attempt to use figurative language?

- Does the student recognize and correct misspelled words?

continues

TEACHER CONFERENCE NOTE *continued*

Support the students by asking questions such as:

Q *I notice that you changed these words. Why did you decide to make this change?*

Q *Listen as I read this line of your poem to you. What did you imagine as you heard that line? What descriptive words might you add to that line to help the reader imagine?*

Q *Where will you look to find the correct spelling for the words you've circled?*

Document your observations using the "Conference Notes" record sheet (BLM1).

Signal to let the students know when writing time is over.

SHARING AND REFLECTING

 ### Reflect on Making Changes to Poems

Ask and briefly discuss:

Q *What is one change you made to your poem today to get it ready to publish? Tell us about it.*

Collect the students' poems, and tell them they will share them from the Author's Chair tomorrow.

Teacher Note

Prior to Day 4, compile the students' poems into a class book with a cover that includes a title, author information, and an illustration. Alternatively, you might leave the cover blank and ask the students to suggest a title and illustration for it on Day 4.

Day 4

Materials

- Class book of students' poems
- Author's Chair

Publishing

In this lesson, the students:

- Share their poems from the Author's Chair
- Speak clearly and listen to one another
- Express interest in and appreciation for one another's writing
- Write freely

GETTING READY TO SHARE

 Introduce the Class Book

Gather the class with partners sitting together, facing the Author's Chair. Show the cover of the class book, and tell the students that you have collected their poems into this book. Read the title and author information, and discuss the illustration (or discuss as a class what to write and draw on the cover; see the Teacher Note on page 533).

Explain that today the students will read their poems to the class from the Author's Chair; then the book will go into the classroom library so that they and others can read and enjoy the poems.

 Review Speaking Clearly and Listening Respectfully

Briefly review Author's Chair sharing procedures. Then ask and briefly discuss:

Q *Why is it important to speak in a loud, clear voice when you share your poem today?*

Q *If you can't hear the poet, how can you respectfully let him or her know?*

Q *What will you do to let the poet know you are interested in his or her poem?*

Encourage the students to be good listeners during sharing time. Tell them that you will check in with them later to see how they did.

SHARING TIME

3 ▶ Share Poems from the Author's Chair

Call a student to the Author's Chair and have him read his poem (including the title) aloud twice. After the reading, comment on descriptive words or figurative language you noticed in the poem. Then invite the class to comment on the poem by asking questions such as:

Q *What did you like about [Adrian's] poem?*

Q *What descriptive words did you hear in the poem? What did that make you imagine?*

Q *What questions do you want to ask [Adrian] about what [he] wrote?*

Follow the same procedure to have other students share their poems.

REFLECTING

4 ▶ Reflect on Author's Chair Sharing

Ask and briefly discuss:

Q *What did we do well during Author's Chair sharing today?*

Q *If you shared today, how did your classmates make you feel? What did they do that made you feel [happy/nervous/proud]?*

Assure the students that haven't yet shared that they will get to share their poems from the Author's Chair in the coming days.

Teacher Note

◀ Repeat Author's Chair sharing as needed so that all of the students get to share their poems with the class.

FREE WRITING TIME

 Write Freely

Explain that the students will have time now to write freely about anything they choose. They may continue a poem or story they've already started or begin a new one. If they need help thinking of an idea, they may look at the class charts or the writing ideas section of their notebooks. Ask and briefly discuss:

Q *What might you write about today?*

Have a few volunteers share their ideas, and then have the students write freely.

Teacher Note

This is the last week of the unit. Students will stay with their current partner for Unit 7.

Clouds

by Christina G. Rossetti

White sheep, white sheep
On a blue hill,
When the wind stops
You all stand still.
When the wind blows
You walk away slow.
White sheep, white sheep,
Where do you go?

Rain Poem
by Elizabeth Coatsworth

The rain was like a little mouse,
quiet, small and gray.
It pattered all around the house
and then it went away.

It did not come, I understand,
indoors at all, until
it found an open window and
left tracks across the sill.

Poetry

The Steam Shovel

by Rowena Bennett

The steam digger
Is much bigger
Than the biggest beast I know.
He snorts and roars
Like the dinosaurs
That lived long years ago.

He crouches low
On his tractor paws
And scoops the dirt up
With his jaws;
Then swings his long
Stiff neck around
And spits it out
Upon the ground…

Oh, the steam digger
Is much bigger
Than the biggest beast I know.
He snorts and roars
Like the dinosaurs
That lived long years ago.

Unit 7

Revisiting the Writing Community

Unit 7

Revisiting the Writing Community

During this final week of the *Being a Writer* program, the students reflect on what they enjoyed about writing this year and on their growth as writers and members of the writing community. They think about writing they might do during the summer and learn more about the writing habits of professional authors. They reflect on how they built a caring community of writers and write letters to next year's class about how to work well together. They consider their relationships to others, build on one another's thinking, and express interest in one another's writing.

UNIT OVERVIEW

WEEK	DAY 1	DAY 2	DAY 3	DAY 4
1	**Reflecting on Writing** Focus: • Discussing what they liked about writing time • Writing about writing time • Sharing their writing from the Author's Chair	**Reflecting on Writing** Focus: • Reading their writing and selecting favorite pieces • Reflecting on how their writing has changed • Sharing their writing from the Author's Chair	**Planning for Summer Writing** Focus: • Learning about the writing habits of professional authors • Making plans for writing in the summer	**Reflecting on Community** Focus: • Discussing how they worked well together • Writing letters to next year's class about how to work well together

Week 1 Overview

UNIT 7: REVISITING THE WRITING COMMUNITY

Excerpts

"Writing Habits of Professional Authors"
(see page 562)

Four writers discuss habits that help them write.

Writing Focus

- Students write about what they liked about writing time this year.

- Students reflect on their growth as writers.

- Students learn about the writing habits of professional authors.

- Students plan summer writing.

- Students write letters to next year's class about the writing community.

Social Focus

- Students reflect on the writing community.

- Students reflect on their relationships to others.

- Students build on one another's thinking.

- Students express interest in and appreciation for one another's writing.

DO AHEAD

- Prior to Day 1, display a few of the books the students have heard during the *Being a Writer* program this year. Also display any class books of student writing you have from the year.

- Prior to Day 2, gather three pieces of writing by each student—one from the beginning of the year, one from the middle of the year, and one from the end of the year. Include work from disassembled class books, as well as other pieces. (See "About Collecting Samples of Student Writing" on page 550.)

TEACHER AS WRITER

"Growth is exciting; growth is dynamic and alarming. Growth of the soul, growth of the mind."
— *Vita Sackville-West*

Reflect this week on your development as a writer and teacher of writing. What growth have you observed in yourself as a writer and writing teacher? In what ways do you hope to grow in the future? Jot down your thoughts and feelings in your writing notebook and date your entry. Continue to write in your notebook during the summer and in the coming year.

Day 1

Materials

- Read-aloud books from earlier in the program (see "Do Ahead" on page 545)
- Any class books from the year (see "Do Ahead" on page 545)
- *Assessment Resource Book*
- Author's Chair

Reflecting on Writing

In this lesson, the students:

- Discuss what they liked about writing time this year
- Write about writing time
- Imagine and discuss how others might feel
- Ask one another questions about their writing

GETTING READY TO WRITE

1 ▎ Reflect on Writing This Year

Teacher Note ▶

You will not assign new partners this week. Have the students work with their Unit 6 partner or with someone sitting near them.

Gather the class with partners sitting together, facing you. Explain that during this last week of the *Being a Writer* program the students will think about what they've enjoyed about writing this year and how they've grown as writers and members of the writing community. Explain that they will also talk about writing they might do this summer.

Review that during writing time this year the students did many things that helped them become stronger writers. Direct their attention to the display of read-aloud books. Remind them that they heard many examples of good writing and learned where authors get ideas and what they do to make their writing interesting and fun to read. Read two or three of the titles aloud and briefly talk about each book.

Point to any class books you have displayed and read a few of the titles aloud. Remind the students that they wrote many stories, nonfiction pieces, letters, and poems this year.

Review that the students also worked with many different partners, talking about their ideas, helping each other improve their writing,

Teacher Note

You might say, "We read *'Let's Get a PUP!' Said Kate* and found out that authors tell more in their stories by adding details that help us imagine or get to know the characters better. We read *Koko's Kitten* and learned that authors of nonfiction write about subjects of interest to them, ask themselves questions, look for answers, and write about what they find out."

and sometimes writing together. They also shared their writing with
their partners as well as sharing from the Author's Chair.

Use "Think, Pair, Share" to have partners first think about and
then discuss:

 Q *What did you like best about writing this year?* [pause] *Turn to
your partner.*

When most pairs have finished talking, signal for the students'
attention and have a few volunteers share their thinking with the class.

> ***Students might say:***
>
> "I liked writing fiction stories, especially ones about space aliens."
>
> "I liked writing poems and making up funny words."
>
> "I think talking with my partner was the best thing."
>
> "Author's Chair sharing was my favorite part."

2 ▶ Think Before Writing

Explain that today the students will write about what they liked
best about writing this year. Remind the students that this year they
learned that good writers think about what they will write before
they write. Ask:

 Q *What will you write about during writing time today? Turn to
your partner.*

Signal for the students' attention. Explain that after writing time
today, they will have a chance to share their writing from the
Author's Chair.

WRITING TIME

3 ▶ Write About Writing

Have the students return to their seats and write in their notebooks
for 15–20 minutes about what they liked about writing this year.

Encourage students who finish early to tell more by adding to their writing. As they work, circulate and observe.

> ### CLASS ASSESSMENT NOTE
>
> As you observe the students, ask yourself:
>
> * Are the students writing with confidence and enthusiasm?
>
> * Does their writing make sense?
>
> * Do they add to their writing to tell more?
>
> * Do they capitalize and punctuate sentences correctly?
>
> * Do they capitalize proper nouns and the pronoun *I*?
>
> * Do they approximate spelling and use the word wall?
>
> Record your observations in the *Assessment Resource Book.*

Signal to let the students know when writing time is over.

SHARING AND REFLECTING

4 ▶ Reflect on How Others Might Feel

Gather the class with the students sitting and facing the Author's Chair. Have them bring their writing with them. Explain that some of them will share their writing from the Author's Chair. Ask and briefly discuss:

Q *What can we do to be a respectful audience when someone is sharing?*

Q *How do you think that will make the author feel?*

Students might say:

"We can listen."

"We can tell the author what we liked about her writing."

"It will make the author feel happy."

Share from the Author's Chair

Call on a student to share her writing from the Author's Chair. After the student has shared, allow her to call on two or three students who would like to comment on her writing. If necessary, ask the class:

Q *What did you find out by listening to [Madison's] writing?*

Q *What questions can we ask [Madison] about [her] writing?*

Follow this same procedure to have more students share from the Author's Chair.

◀ **Teacher Note**

More students will have an opportunity to share from the Author's Chair on Day 2.

 Reflect on Author's Chair Sharing

Ask and briefly discuss:

Q *What did we do to show the authors who shared today that we were interested in their writing?*

Q *What problems did we have? What can we do next time to avoid those problems?*

Explain that tomorrow the students will think more about the writing they have done this year.

Day 2

Materials

- Three samples of each student's writing (see "Do Ahead" on page 545)
- Author's Chair

Reflecting on Writing

In this lesson, the students:

- Review some pieces of writing from this year
- Select favorite pieces to share
- Reflect on how they benefit from the writing community
- Consider the impact of their behavior on others
- Ask one another questions about their writing
- Write freely

About Collecting Samples of Student Writing

Today the students will reread three pieces they wrote this year and think about how their writing has changed and how they have grown as writers. Select final versions of pieces from the beginning, middle, and end of the year that clearly illustrate growth in the students' writing. If possible, use the same pieces for all of the students, for example, you might select the stories about places they like to go from Unit 1, Week 1; the published fiction pieces from Unit 3; and the published poems from Unit 6.

GETTING READY TO SHARE

 1 Read and Select Favorite Pieces of Writing

Have partners sit together at desks today. Remind them that yesterday they wrote about what they liked best about writing time this year. Explain that today they will look at some of the writing they did this year and think about how they have changed and grown as writers.

Tell the students that you will give them each three pieces of their own writing—one from the beginning of the year, one from the middle of the year, and one they wrote recently—and briefly explain what each piece is. Explain that you would like them to read each piece quietly to themselves and then decide which piece they like best and why.

Distribute the pieces and give the students time to read each one.
Then ask:

 Q *Which piece of writing do you like the best and why? Turn to
your partner.*

Signal for the students' attention and have a few volunteers share
their thinking with the class.

> ***Students might say:***
>
> "I like the piece I wrote about the place I like to go. I still like to go
> to that place."
>
> "I like the fiction story I wrote because it has good descriptions."
>
> "I like the poem I wrote about the tree in the courtyard because I
> think I used interesting words like 'sparkly wet leaves' and 'rough
> brown trunk.'"

2 ▶ Think About How Their Writing Has Changed

Remind the students that they have examples of their writing from
the beginning, middle, and end of the year. Ask them to read each
of these pieces again and see what they notice about how their
writing has changed over the year.

Give the students a few minutes to reread their writing. Then ask:

 Q *What do you notice about how your writing has changed this
year? Turn to your partner.*

Signal for the students' attention and have a few volunteers share
their thinking with the class.

> ***Students might say:***
>
> "I didn't write very much at the beginning of the year. Now I write
> a lot."
>
> "I write more description in my stories and poems now, so people
> can picture them in their minds."
>
> "I didn't know how to write poems before. Now I do."
>
> "I know how to spell more words, and I know how to use an
> exclamation point."

Teacher Note ▶

You might say, "I've noticed that you write much more now than you did at the beginning of the year, and you use descriptive words in your writing. I've also noticed that you have many good writing ideas, and that you use ideas you've collected in your writing notebooks. In addition, I notice that you write fiction, nonfiction, letters, and poems."

Share some of your own observations about changes you've noticed in the students' writing and how they have grown as writers.

Tell the students that you appreciate the hard work they've done this year to become stronger writers.

SHARING AND REFLECTING

▶ **3** **Consider the Impact of Their Behavior on Others**

Gather the class with the students sitting and facing the Author's Chair. Have them bring the piece of writing they like best with them. Explain that they will share their writing from the Author's Chair. Ask and briefly discuss:

Q *What can authors who share today do to help us hear their writing?*

Q *Why is it important to help the audience hear what you've written?*

Tell the students to keep these ideas in mind as they share their writing from the Author's Chair today.

▶ **4** **Share from the Author's Chair**

Call on a student to share his writing from the Author's Chair. After the student has shared, allow him to call on two or three students who would like to comment on his writing. If necessary, ask the class:

Q *What did you find out by listening to [Terry's] writing?*

Q *What questions can we ask [Terry] about [his] writing?*

Teacher Note ▶

If necessary, plan more sharing time so all of the students can share their writing from the Author's Chair.

Follow this same procedure to have more students share from the Author's Chair.

5 ▸ Reflect on Author's Chair Sharing

Ask and briefly discuss:

Q *What did the authors who shared their writing today do to help us hear them?*

Q *What do you like about sharing your writing with the writing community?*

Q *How does sharing your writing with the writing community help you become a stronger writer?*

Explain that tomorrow the students will think about writing they might do this summer.

FREE WRITING TIME

6 ▸ Write Freely

Explain that the students will now have time to write freely about any topic they choose. Discuss:

Q *What is something you might write about today?*

Have the students write freely.

Day 3

Materials

- "Writing Habits of Professional Authors" (see page 562)
- Highlighter or marker for each student

Planning for Summer Writing

In this lesson, the students:

- Learn about the writing practices of professional authors
- Plan for summer writing
- Ask one another questions about their writing
- Get ideas by listening to one another

GETTING READY TO WRITE

▶1 **Identify and List Summer Writing Topics**

Gather the class with partners sitting together, facing you. Have them bring their notebooks with them.

Review that this week the students looked back at their writing experiences and thought about the things they enjoyed about writing and how they have grown as writers this year. Explain that today they will look ahead and plan how they will keep writing this summer.

Ask the students to open to the writing ideas section of their notebooks and review the ideas they've listed. After a minute or two, signal for the students' attention and use "Think, Pair, Share" to have partners first think about and then discuss:

 Q *What are some ideas on your list that you didn't write about this year that you are still interested in writing about?* [pause] *Turn to your partner.*

After a moment, signal for the students' attention. Distribute a highlighter or marker to each student and explain that you would like them to highlight or mark the ideas they might write about this summer. Allow a few minutes for them to do so; then ask:

 Q *What else could you write about this summer? Turn to your partner.*

After a moment, signal for the students' attention. Have them turn to the next empty page in the writing ideas section and jot down any new ideas they have for their summer writing.

When most students have finished writing, ask and discuss as a class:

Q *What are some things you might write about this summer?*

Q *Why do you think it is important to keep writing during the summer?*

> **Students might say:**
>
> "It's important to keep writing so we won't forget how to be a good writer."
>
> "I agree with [Justin] and in addition, it will help us get even better at writing."
>
> "There's a lot to write about in the summer."

▶2 Read and Discuss Authors' Writing Habits

Explain that many authors have daily habits that help them keep writing. They might have a special time or place they write, and they might write for a certain length of time. Sometimes they use particular materials, like a favorite kind of pen or paper. Explain that today you will read some quotes by professional authors about their writing habits. Ask the students to think about writing habits they might establish for themselves at home this summer.

Read "Writing Habits of Professional Authors" aloud, clarifying vocabulary as you read.

> **Suggested Vocabulary**
>
> **teak:** kind of wood
> **legal pads:** tablets of writing paper
> **draftsman:** someone who draws plans for buildings, ships, aircraft, or machines
> **limber:** easily bent, flexible

◀ **Teacher Note**

Support struggling students by asking them questions, such as:

Q *What is something you like to do that you might write about?*

Q *What do you wonder about third grade? What might you write about that?*

Q *Who is someone you might write a letter to?*

Q *What do you hope to do this summer? What might you write about that?*

Ask and briefly discuss:

Q *What writing habits help these authors?*

Q *What habits might help you write this summer?*

Teacher Note ▶

If the students struggle with this question, stimulate their thinking by asking questions, such as:

Q *How often might you write this summer?*

Q *At what time of day might you write?*

Q *Where might you write?*

Q *What writing materials might you use?*

WRITING TIME

3 Write About Writing Habits

Explain that during writing time today, the students will write about specific habits they want to establish this summer, such as where and when they will write, how often and for how long, and what writing materials they will use. Tell them that if they finish, they may add to their list of topics to write about this summer or choose one of those ideas and write about it.

Have the students return to their seats and write silently for 20–30 minutes.

Signal to let the students know when writing time is over.

SHARING AND REFLECTING

4 Share Plans for Summer Writing

Ask the students to read what they wrote today and underline a sentence that tells one thing they will do to help them write this summer. Give them a moment to select a sentence, and then have each student read his sentence aloud to the class, without comment.

When all of the students have read their sentences, ask and briefly discuss as a class:

Q *What ideas did you hear that you want to add to your summer writing plans?*

Q *What questions do you want to ask a classmate about the sentence he or she shared?*

Give the students a moment to add any new ideas to their notebooks, if they wish. Encourage them to continue writing as much as they can this summer and to focus on enjoying their own writing.

EXTENSION

Write Letters Home

To further promote summer writing, consider one or more of the following activities:

- As a class, write a letter to parents explaining the importance of summer writing and encouraging them to create time for their child to write during the summer. Copy the letter for each student to take home.

- Have the students write individual letters to their own parents explaining the importance of summer writing and the habits they wish to establish for themselves.

- Have the students write letters to themselves describing their summer writing plans. Have them put the letters in envelopes addressed to themselves. Mail the letters to the students so that they receive them a few weeks after vacation begins.

Day 4

Materials

- Chart paper and a marker
- Loose, lined paper or stationery for each student
- *Assessment Resource Book*

Reflecting on Community

In this lesson, the students:

- Reflect on how they worked together to build the writing community
- Write letters to next year's class about working well together
- Reflect on their contributions to the writing community

GETTING READY TO WRITE

Making Meaning® Teacher

Some questions in this lesson are similar to questions asked in the last week of the *Making Meaning* program. Read the lessons in both programs and decide if you want to teach them separately or combine them into one lesson.

▶1 Introduce Writing About the Writing Community

Gather the class with partners sitting together, facing you. Remind the students that they have worked hard this year to build a caring writing community in which they helped one another. Explain that today they will each write a letter to next year's second grade class about how to work together during writing time. Explain that next year's second graders can read the letters and learn what they can do to build a caring writing community.

▶2 Generate Ideas to Include in Letters

Use "Think, Pair, Share" to have the students first think about and then discuss:

Teacher Note

You might share a few ideas to stimulate the students' thinking and encourage them to phrase their ideas in a positive way, for example, "It is polite to look at people when they are talking. It is fun to share ideas with your partner."

Q *What advice would you give next year's second grade class about working together during writing time?* [pause] *Turn to your partner.*

Q *What else do you want next year's second graders to know about writing time?* [pause] *Turn to your partner.*

For each question, have several volunteers share their thinking. As they share their ideas, record them on a sheet of chart paper entitled "Ideas for Letters to Second Graders." If necessary, prompt the students' thinking with questions such as:

Q *What is important to do when you work with a partner?*

Q *What is important to do during a whole class discussion?*

Q *What did we do this year to be good listeners?*

Q *What is something that you know next year's second graders will enjoy during writing time?*

Ideas for Letters to Second Graders

- Turn and look at the person who is talking.
- If you can't hear, ask the person who is talking to speak up.
- Make sure you have everyone's attention before you talk.
- Take turns with your partner.
- Share your writing from the Author's Chair.
- Have pair conferences.
- Make your own books.

Explain that each student will write a letter to next year's second graders during writing time today. Explain that these letters will be collected in a book entitled "The Writing Community in Second Grade," and that the book will be given to next year's class. Explain that the letters they write today will be the final versions, so they should use their best handwriting and try to make their letters as free of errors as possible.

WRITING TIME

3 **Write Letters to Next Year's Second Grade Class**

Distribute lined writing paper or stationery to the students, and have them return to their seats. Have them work on their letters for 20–30 minutes. Remind them to look at the "Ideas for Letters to Second Graders" chart to help them get ideas. As the students work, circulate and observe.

CLASS ASSESSMENT NOTE

Observe the students and notice whether the majority of the students incorporate the skills learned this year as they write letters on their own. Ask yourself:

* Do the students remember to include the five parts of a letter?

* Do they punctuate their letters appropriately?

* Do their letters make sense and communicate clearly?

* Do they check their spelling and make necessary corrections?

Record your observations in the *Assessment Resource Book*.

Signal to let the students know when writing time is over.

SHARING AND REFLECTING

4 **Share Letters in Pairs**

Gather the class with partners sitting together, facing you. Have them bring their letters with them. Have partners read their letters to each other; then signal for the students' attention and ask:

Q *How is your partner's letter similar to yours? How are the letters different?*

Collect the students' letters.

Reflect on Growth as Caring Community Members

Share some observations about ways your students have grown as members of the writing community this year. Then ask:

Q *What else have you done to be a caring member of our writing community?*

Encourage the students to continue to write over the summer and to become caring members of their classroom writing community next year. Have the students take a moment to thank one another for their work together during writing time this year.

◀ **Teacher Note**

You might say, "I remember that at the beginning of the year some people didn't listen to their partner when they shared ideas. Now I see you looking at your partner and nodding when you share your thinking. That shows me that you have learned how to listen respectfully to each other. I also remember that some people had trouble working quietly during writing time at the beginning of the year. Now you get to work right away and write silently the entire time."

Teacher Note

Compile the students' letters into a class book entitled *The Writing Community in Second Grade*, and plan to share the book with your incoming class this fall.

Excerpts

Writing Habits of Professional Authors

"…I try to write every day. It's like physical exercise…if you just do it once a week, it's not going to be as good as if you do it every day…."

— Max Apple

"I generally write for three or four hours at a sitting, mornings as a rule."

— Saul Bellow

"Have some sort of private place to work in. Put up a sign to keep from being interrupted. Mine says: 'PLEASE, do *not* knock, do *not* say hello or goodbye, do *not* ask what's for dinner, do *not* disturb me unless the police or firemen have to be called.'"

— Judith Krantz

"I have a nice teak desk, long and wide, on which I keep special things: crisp new legal pads and No. 2 pencils with good rubber erasers that don't leave red smears; a dark blue draftsman lamp that twists and bends like a tall, limber skeleton; a small quartz clock that silently flicks the minutes…and an orange tomcat who lies on a blanket and snores."

— Gail Godwin

Appendices

Grade 2 Skill Development Chart

X = skill taught/practiced

Prewriting	Drafting	Revision	Proofreading	Publication	Writing Process: / Skill code	Capitalize the first letters of sentences and use periods at the ends	Approximate spelling of single-syllable words	Approximate spelling of polysyllabic words	Use a word wall to spell high-frequency sight words	Use a personal word bank to proofread spelling	Capitalize proper nouns and *I*	Use commas in a series	Use quotation marks to punctuate speech	Use commas in the date, greeting, and closing of letters
X	X			X	2.1.1									
X	X			X	2.1.2									
X	X			X	2.1.3	X								
X	X			X	2.1.4	X	X							
X	X				2.1.5	X	X				X			
X	X			X	2.1.6	X	X		X		X			
X	X			X	2.1.7	X	X		X		X			
X	X				2.2.1	X	X		X		X			
X	X			X	2.2.2	X	X		X		X	X		
X	X				2.2.3	X	X		X		X	X		
X	X			X	2.2.4	X	X		X		X	X		
X	X				2.3.1	X	X		X		X		X	
X	X				2.3.2	X			X	X	X		X	
X	X	X	X		2.3.3	X	X		X	X	X		X	
X	X			X	2.3.4	X			X	X	X		X	
X	X				2.4.1	X			X		X			
X	X				2.4.2	X			X		X			
X	X				2.4.3	X			X		X			
X	X				2.4.4	X			X		X			
X	X	X	X	X	2.4.5	X			X	X	X			
X	X				2.5.1	X			X		X			
X	X	X	X	X	2.5.2	X			X		X			X
X	X	X	X	X	2.5.3	X			X	X	X			X
X	X				2.6.1	X			X		X			
X	X				2.6.2	X			X		X			
X	X	X	X	X	2.6.3	X			X	X	X			
X	X	X	X	X	2.7.1	X			X		X			X

Bibliography

Ainsworth, Mary. "Patterns of Attachment Behaviour Shown by the Infant in Interaction with His Mother." *Merrill-Palmer Quarterly* 10 (1964): 51–58.

Anderson, Richard C., and P. David Pearson. "A Schema-Theoretic View of Basic Process in Reading Comprehension." In *Handbook of Reading Research* edited by P. David Pearson. New York: Longman, 1984.

Asher, James J. "Children Learning Another Language: A Developmental Hypothesis." *Child Development* 48 (1977): 1040–48.

———. "Children's First Language as a Model for Second Language Learning." *Modern Language Journal* 56 (1972): 133–39.

———. "The Strategy of Total Physical Response: An Application to Learning Russian." *International Review of Applied Linguistics* 3 (1965): 291–300.

Atwell, Nancie. *In the Middle: New Understandings About Writing, Reading, and Learning*. Portsmouth, NH: Heinemann-Boynton/Cook, 1998.

Battistich, Victor, Daniel Solomon, Dong-il Kim, Marilyn Watson, and Eric Schaps. "Schools as Communities, Poverty Levels of Student Populations, and Students' Attitudes, Motives, and Performance: A Multilevel Analysis." *American Educational Research Journal* 32, no. 3 (Fall 1995): 627–58.

Beck, Isabel L., Margaret G. McKeown, and Linda Kucan. *Bringing Words to Life: Robust Vocabulary Instruction*. New York: Guilford Press, 2002.

Bowlby, John. *Attachment and Loss*. Vol. 1, *Attachment*. New York: Basic Books, 1997.

Calkins, Lucy. *The Art of Teaching Writing*. Portsmouth, NH: Heinemann, 1994.

Contestable, Julie W., Shaila Regan, Susie Alldredge, Carol Westrich, and Laurel Robertson. *Number Power: A Cooperative Approach to Mathematics and Social Development Grades K–6*. Oakland, CA: Developmental Studies Center, 1999.

Culham, Ruth. *6+1 Traits of Writing: The Complete Guide for the Primary Grades*. Portland, OR: Northwest Regional Educational Laboratory, 2005.

———. *6+1 Traits of Writing: The Complete Guide, Grades 3 and Up*. Portland, OR: Northwest Regional Educational Laboratory, 2003.

Cummins, James. "The Role of Primary Language Development in Promoting Educational Success for Language Minority Students." In *Schooling and Language Minority Students: A Theoretical Framework*. Los Angeles: California State University, Evaluation, Dissemination, and Assessment Center, 1981.

Cunningham, Anne E., and Keith E. Stanovich. "What Reading Does for the Mind." *American Educator*, Spring/Summer 1998, 8–15.

Developmental Studies Center. *Blueprints for a Collaborative Classroom*. Oakland, CA: Developmental Studies Center, 1997.

———. *Ways We Want Our Class to Be*. Oakland, CA: Developmental Studies Center, 1996.

DeVries, Rheta, and Betty Zan. *Moral Classrooms, Moral Children*. New York: Teachers College Press, 1994.

Dewey, John. *Democracy and Education*. New York: Macmillan, 1916.

Fletcher, Ralph, and JoAnn Portalupi. *Writing Workshop: The Essential Guide*. Portsmouth, NH: Heinemann, 2001.

Flood, James, Dianne Lapp, and Julie M. Jensen. *The Handbook of Research on Teaching the English Language*. Mahwah, NJ: Lawrence Erlbaum Associates, 2002.

Freedman, Sarah W., Linda Flower, Glynda Hull, and J. R. Hayes. "Ten Years of Research: Achievements of the National Center for the Study of Writing and Literacy." In *A Handbook for Literacy Educators: Research on Teaching the Communicative and Visual Arts*, edited by J. Flood, S. B. Heath, and D. Lapp. Forthcoming.

Gambrell, Linda B., Lesley Mandel Morrow, Susan B. Neuman, and Michael Pressley, eds. *Best Practices in Literacy Instruction*. New York: Guilford Press, 1999.

Graves, Donald H. "Children Can Write Authentically If We Help Them." *Primary Voices K–6* 1, no. 1 (2003): 2–6.

Graves, Donald H. *Writing: Teachers and Children at Work*. Portsmouth, NH: Heinemann, 2003.

Hakuta, Kenji, Yuko Goto Butler, and Daria Witt. *How Long Does It Take English Learners to Attain Proficiency?* Santa Barbara, CA: University of California, Linguistic Minority Research Institute, 2000.

Harvey, Stephanie. *Nonfiction Matters: Reading, Writing, and Research in Grades 3–8*. York, ME: Stenhouse Publishers, 1998.

Herrell, Adrienne L. *Fifty Strategies for Teaching English Language Learners*. Upper Saddle River, NJ: Merrill, 2000.

Johnson, David W., Roger T. Johnson, and Edythe Johnson Holubec. *The New Circles of Learning: Cooperation in the Classroom*. Alexandria, VA: Association for Supervision and Curriculum Development, 1994.

Kagan, Spencer. *Cooperative Learning*. San Juan Capistrano, CA: Resources of Teachers, 1992.

Kamil, Michael L., Peter B. Mosenthal, P. David Pearson, and Rebecca Barr, eds. *Handbook of Reading Research, Volume III*. Mahwah, NJ: Lawrence Erlbaum Associates, 2000.

Kelley, Michael C. *Teachers' Reports of Writing Instruction at a High Performing Elementary School*. University of Delaware: Doctoral dissertation, 2002.

Kohlberg, Lawrence. *The Psychology of Moral Development*. New York: Harper and Row, 1984.

Kohn, Alfie. *Beyond Discipline: From Compliance to Community*. Alexandria, VA: Association for Supervision and Curriculum Development, 1996.

————. *Punished by Rewards: The Trouble with Gold Stars, Incentive Plans, A's, Praise, and Other Bribes*. New York: Houghton Mifflin Company, 1999.

Krashen, Stephen D. *Principles and Practice in Second Language Acquisition*. New York: Prentice-Hall, 1982.

————. *Second Language Acquisition and Second Language Learning*. New York: Pergamon Press, 1981.

————. "TPR: Still a Very Good Idea." *NovELTy* 5, no. 4 (1998).

————, and Tracy D. Terrell. *The Natural Approach: Language Acquisition in the Classroom*. Englewood Cliffs, NJ: Prentice Hall, 1983.

National Commission on Writing in America's Colleges and Schools. *The Neglected "R": The Need for a Writing Revolution*. New York: College Board, 2003.

National Council of Teachers of English. *What We Know About Writing: Early Literacy*. NCTE Writing Initiative. www.ncte.org/prog/writing/research/113328.htm.

National Governor's Association for Best Practices. *Making Writing Instruction Work*. Washington, DC: National Governor's Association Center for Best Practices, 2001.

Nucci, Larry P., ed. *Moral Development and Character Education: A Dialogue*. Berkeley, CA: McCutchan Publishing Corporation, 1989.

Optiz, Michael F., ed. *Literacy Instruction for Culturally and Linguistically Diverse Students*. Newark, DE: International Reading Association, 1998.

Piaget, Jean. *The Child's Conception of the World*. Trans. Joan and Andrew Tomlinson. Lanham, MD: Littlefield Adams, 1969.

———. *The Moral Judgment of the Child*. Trans. Marjorie Gabain. New York: The Free Press, 1965.

Ray, Katie Wood. *About the Authors: Writing Workshop with Our Youngest Writers*. Portsmouth, NH: Heinemann, 2004.

Resnick, Michael D., P. S. Bearman, R. W. Blum, K. E. Bauman, K. M. Harris, J. Jones, J. Tabor, et al. "Protecting Adolescents from Harm: Findings from the National Longitudinal Study on Adolescent Health." *Journal of the American Medical Association* 278 (1997): 823–32.

Schaps, Eric, Victor Battistich, and Dan Solomon. "Community in School a Key to Student Growth: Findings from the Child Development Project." In *Building School Success on Social and Emotional Learning*, edited by R. Weissberg, J. Zins, and H. Walbert. New York: Teachers College Press, 2004.

Schaps, Eric, Catherine Lewis, and Marilyn Watson. "Building Classroom Communities." *Thrust for Educational Leadership*, September 1997.

Schaps, Eric, Esther F. Schaeffer, and Sanford N. McDonnell. "What's Right and Wrong in Character Education Today." *Education Week*, September 12, 2001: 40–44.

Shefelbine, John, and Katherine K. Newman. *SIPPS: Systematic Instruction in Phoneme Awareness, Phonics, and Sight Words*. Oakland, CA: Developmental Studies Center, 2005.

Sulzby, Elizabeth. "Research Directions: Transitions from Emergent to Conventional Writing." *Language Arts* 69 (1992): 290–97.

Swain, M., and S. Lapkin. "Problems in Output and the Cognitive Processes They Generate: A Step Toward Second Language Learning." *Applied Linguistics* 16, no. 3 (1995): 371–91.

William, Joan A. "Classroom Conversations: Opportunities to Learn for ESL Students in Mainstream Classrooms." *The Reading Teacher* 54, no. 8 (2001): 750–57.

Blackline Masters

Unpunctuated Letter 1

February 14 2010

Dear Pat

I am glad that you are my friend we have fun when we

play together I hope you get lots of valentines today

Your friend

Terry

Unpunctuated Letter 2

February 15 2010

Dear Terry

Thank you for your letter I did get lots of valentines I like to play with you too let's go to the park after school today

Your friend

Pat

© Developmental Studies Center Being a Writer™ | **BLM5**

from *First Year Letters* by Julie Danneberg

Being a Writer.
Reorder Information

Kindergarten

Complete Classroom Package — BW-CPK-REV

Contents: Teacher's Manual (2 volumes), 25 dry-erase markers and wipe-off boards, and 19 trade books.

Available separately

Teacher's Manual, vol. 1	BW-TMK-V1-REV
Teacher's Manual, vol. 2	BW-TMK-V2
Dry-erase markers and wipe-off boards (25 of each)	BW-DEPKG
Trade book set (19 books)	BW-TBSK

Grade 1

Complete Classroom Package — BW-CP1-REV

Contents: Teacher's Manual (2 volumes), Assessment Resource Book, 25 dry-erase markers and wipe-off boards, and 21 trade books.

Available separately

Teacher's Manual, vol. 1	BW-TM1-V1-REV
Teacher's Manual, vol. 2	BW-TM1-V2
Assessment Resource Book	BW-AB1-REV
CD-ROM Grade 1 Reproducible Materials	BW-CDR1-REV
Dry-erase markers and wipe-off boards (25 of each)	BW-DEPKG
Trade book set (21 books)	BW-TBS1

Grade 2

Complete Classroom Package — BW-CP2

Contents: Teacher's Manual (2 volumes), Skill Practice Teaching Guide, Assessment Resource Book, 25 Student Writing Handbooks, 25 Student Skill Practice Books, and 27 trade books.

Available separately

Teacher's Manual, vol. 1	BW-TM2-V1
Teacher's Manual, vol. 2	BW-TM2-V2
Skill Practice Teaching Guide	BW-STG2
Assessment Resource Book	BW-AB2
Student Writing Handbook pack (5 books)	BW-SB2-Q5
Student Skill Practice Book pack (5 books)	BW-SSB2-Q5
CD-ROM Grade 2 Reproducible Materials	BW-CDR2
Trade book set (27 books)	BW-TBS2

Grade 3

Complete Classroom Package — BW-CP3

Contents: Teacher's Manual (2 volumes), Skill Practice Teaching Guide, Assessment Resource Book, 25 Student Writing Handbooks, 25 Student Skill Practice Books, and 33 trade books.

Available separately

Teacher's Manual, vol. 1	BW-TM3-V1
Teacher's Manual, vol. 2	BW-TM3-V2
Skill Practice Teaching Guide	BW-STG3
Assessment Resource Book	BW-AB3
Student Writing Handbook pack (5 books)	BW-SB3-Q5
Student Skill Practice Book pack (5 books)	BW-SSB3-Q5
CD-ROM Grade 3 Reproducible Materials	BW-CDR3
Trade book set (33 books)	BW-TBS3

Grade 4

Complete Classroom Package — BW-CP4

Contents: Teacher's Manual (2 volumes), Skill Practice Teaching Guide, Assessment Resource Book, 30 Student Writing Handbooks, 30 Student Skill Practice Books, and 25 trade books.

Available separately

Teacher's Manual, vol. 1	BW-TM4-V1
Teacher's Manual, vol. 2	BW-TM4-V2
Skill Practice Teaching Guide	BW-STG4
Assessment Resource Book	BW-AB4
Student Writing Handbook pack (5 books)	BW-SB4-Q5
Student Skill Practice Book pack (5 books)	BW-SSB4-Q5
CD-ROM Grade 4 Reproducible Materials	BW-CDR4
Trade book set (25 books)	BW-TBS4

Grade 5

Complete Classroom Package — BW-CP5

Contents: Teacher's Manual (2 volumes), Skill Practice Teaching Guide, Assessment Resource Book, 30 Student Writing Handbooks, 30 Student Skill Practice Books, and 25 trade books.

Available separately

Teacher's Manual, vol. 1	BW-TM5-V1
Teacher's Manual, vol. 2	BW-TM5-V2
Skill Practice Teaching Guide	BW-STG5
Assessment Resource Book	BW-AB5
Student Writing Handbook pack (5 books)	BW-SB5-Q5
Student Skill Practice Book pack (5 books)	BW-SSB5-Q5
CD-ROM Grade 5 Reproducible Materials	BW-CDR5
Trade book set (25 books)	BW-TBS5

Grade 6

Complete Classroom Package — BW-CP6

Contents: Teacher's Manual (2 volumes), Skill Practice Teaching Guide, Assessment Resource Book, 30 Student Writing Handbooks (2 volumes), 30 Student Skill Practice Books, and 14 trade books.

Available separately

Teacher's Manual, vol. 1	BW-TM6-V1
Teacher's Manual, vol. 2	BW-TM6-V2
Skill Practice Teaching Guide	BW-STG6
Assessment Resource Book	BW-AB6
Student Writing Handbook pack (5 books)	BW-SB6-Q5
Student Skill Practice Book pack (5 books)	BW-SSB6-Q5
CD-ROM Grade 6 Reproducible Materials	BW-CDR6
Trade book set (14 books)	BW-TBS6

Additional genre units are available at grades 3–6. Visit www.devstu.org for more information.

DEVELOPMENTAL STUDIES CENTER.

Ordering Information: To order call 800.666.7270 * fax 510.842.0348 * log on to www.devstu.org * e-mail pubs@devstu.org

Or Mail Your Order to: Developmental Studies Center * Publications Department * 2000 Embarcadero, Suite 305 * Oakland, CA 94606-5300